Agricultural Computer
Guide & Directory

Agricultural Computer Guide & Directory

*Here's How to Decide
If a Computer Is in Your Future*

by the staff of
Oppenheimer Industries, Inc.

Order from

THE INTERSTATE
Printers & Publishers, Inc.
Danville, Illinois 61832-0594

Library of Congress Catalog Card No. 83-82985

1 2 3
4 5 6
7 8 9

ISBN 0-8134-2370-8

Oppenheimer Industries, Inc., is a diversified agricultural investment firm with a long history of proven service.

On staff are some 100 agricultural specialists engaged in every aspect of the industry: real estate sales and acquisitions, management and consulting services, livestock programs and financial packaging. Oppenheimer's services cover the full range of agricultural activity.

This handbook is intended as an aid to the prospective buyer or current owner of a small computer to be used in agricultural operations. Its purpose is to provide information about the factors involved in selecting, purchasing, adapting and learning to use the system best suited to his or her particular situation. It is not a recommendation to purchase, or an endorsement of, any of the products mentioned.

It is hoped that the reference material included will be of help to the reader in making informed decisions. However, a few words of explanation are in order.

The products mentioned here provide a representative sampling of the scope and variety of the resources available to the computer operator engaged in farming and ranching enterprises. The inclusion of a specific company's products was determined by its response to a letter requesting information. Those companies supplying detailed information about their sofware, including reasonably current prices, were selected for inclusion in the reference section.

Not included are those companies which were not contacted by mail, those which did not send price ranges, or whose products are still in the developmental stage and thus not available, and those which did not respond. Thus, this book is a representative—but not complete—indication of the available products.

Acknowledgments

This book is the composite effort of many individuals. We would like to thank the following for their contributions to its development.

Coordinator   **William Windhorst**, Manager, Data Processing Department.

Writers   **Brig. Gen. H. L. Oppenheimer**, USMC Ret., Chairman of the Board

William Ball, President

Garrett Cole, Executive Vice President, Gunsight, Inc.

David Workmon, Vice President, Financial Division

Fred Kiewit, Assistant Vice President, Real Estate Brokerage Division

Ricardo Preve, Agricultural Manager, Management and Consulting Department

Sue Toedtmann, Assistant Manager, Data Processing Department

Illustrator   **Debra Pickens**, Administrative Assistant / Property & Listing Development, Real Estate Brokerage Division

Table of Contents

Introduction

by Brig. Gen. H. L. Oppenheimer, USMC Ret.,
Chairman of the Board,
Oppenheimer Industries, Inc.

In 1953, as a lieutenant colonel on the staff of the Marine Corps Educational Center, I was directed to make a study on the possibility of putting the scheduling, assignment of instructors, logistic support, availability of training areas and any other worthwhile data I could think of, on the IBM system then being used at Quantico for payroll, purchasing and the financial record-keeping of the post. This was an old punch card system. If you punched in a man's name and rank, dependents, length of service, allotments, addresses, units, etc., it would print all the payrolls and prepare data for the budgets and records of Marine Headquarters, the Navy Department and eventually the Defense Department. The installation for a 50,000-man post occupied dozens of machines in a large glass-enclosed space and two floors of an office building with hundreds of file drawers and about 80 persons running to and fro. For new changes on an individual man, a new card was punched. Once a month the machine ran a sort, pulled out the old cards, stuck in the new and had a new printout.

The experts figured that the data I wished to insert would take four more machines, 10 more operators and an entire new printout for daily changes. It was decided that it was cheaper for each of the schools to continue with the old hand system, though it took a whole week for the commanding general to find out what was going on. A question like "how many instructors will the Basic School need next week?" would throw the whole place into a tizzy.

Thirty years later it is my guess that all of this information could be handled on computers in a 20-by-20-foot room with six operators and would include all of the file storage for two or three years. Information on the number of instructors, or the projected total of next week's pay for the entire post, could be produced on a display screen and printed in something less than five seconds. Using a military analogy, it would be like comparing a new guided missile with a pre-Revolutionary musket loader or maybe a bow and arrow.

Every business magazine you pick up now is half full of advertising for the 100 computers on the market or some combination of 1,000 associated gadgets for 10,000 software products. An old "punch card" mentality like my own is somewhat bewildered. One's first reaction is to wait till next year, when they'll have something even better or cheaper, or until one's six-year-old grandson gets to third grade, when he can give instruction on it.

While we have one of the major mainframe installations for our corporate business—of which I understand practically nothing except how expensive it is—I am now considering a smaller "home type" for some personal farms and private accounting and record-keeping. It is my understanding that the cost of the computer, display screen, printer, record storage facilities and some other optional gear will run from $5,000 to $15,000. So it's not just an interesting gadget to "snow your neighbors" with and then to let sit idle in the corner. How should my thinking parallel that of a middle-sized (and middle-aged) farmer or rancher who is going through the same thought processes? The very words, "learning a new computer language," immediately give me a migraine headache.

To begin with, if you are running three 10,000-acre crop farms or 20,000 head of breeder cattle plus a 30,000-head feedlot, you already have a computer and all of the qualified personnel for the system. If you have an eight-hour-a-day job earning $1,000 per month and supporting a wife and three kids, with a 50-acre corn patch that you farm after work, you can't afford a computer. This book addresses itself to the farmer in between. The computer has four areas of justification:

1. To save time.

2. To increase accuracy.
3. To improve record-keeping.
4. To make available certain specialized functions such as word-processing, correspondence, printing, or very rapid telephonic receipt or transmission of information with other computers.

Picking certain agricultural functions at random:

1. The computer can record, sort, itemize, total and analyze all of your expenses and cash outlays together with all sales and inputs and come out with a monthly or annual printed record for both your bank balances and your federal and state tax returns.
2. If you input desired quantities of fertilizer, water, feed, supplements for various fields, cattle herds and livestock pens, tied in with comparative prices, it can calculate optimum changes in mix caused by varying weather, labor or price movements.
3. In areas of expensive water, a sophisticated system can monitor levels of moisture in specific areas and turn water on or off, with major cost savings.
4. The computer can keep all of your addresses, telephone numbers and records of past correspondence instantly available on a display screen or printout.
5. In a purebred operation for cattle, hogs, sheep or a dairy, it can keep all of the production, breeding, registration, sales and cost data necessary for culling, herd improvement or tax records.
6. It can hook into telephone systems with crop and market services and give you an instant printout on prices, markets or weather anywhere in the country. This can be tied into inputs on freight rates by rail, truck or barge for decisions on sales, purchases or hedges.
7. It can type letter-perfect and correctly spelled correspondence even if you haven't finished sixth grade. It can send these letters out to 50 persons with you inserting the addresses and a personal touch like "How's Aunt Emily?"
8. A 1-square-foot box of "floppy disks" can store more information than 10 three-drawer file cabinets and can be retrievable instantly.

Farming has become a high-capital input, high-gross, highly leveraged business with a low net. Financial success or failure can depend on a few percentage points. If money costs 12 percent, fertilizer $60 an acre, herbicide $5 and rent $80 on a specific field producing 100 bushels of corn, do you want to put your limited supply of labor and equipment to work here or somewhere else? Is your decision going to be the same if you can hedge at $2.50 a bushel? Where are you if interest rates go down to 2 percent but rents go to $100? If you inherit $50,000, do you want to buy land and save rent, or pay off debt and save interest? Should you spend $30 an acre more on irrigation water and increase production 10 percent? How would that have come out over the last five years on a particular field?

At first glance, one might think this is more appropriate for a Ph.D. dissertation at the local ag college and that it is "fascinating but irrelevant." Not so. In the modern framework of today's agriculture, on $2,000-an-acre land and with $250-an-acre corn production costs, including labor and equipment, in an "average" year a farmer nets 5 percent on the land investment. If the farmer has a $1,000-an-acre mortgage at 14 percent he or she nets zero. On a $1,400 mortgage, the farmer goes broke. A 2 percent decrease in interest rates, a 3 percent increase in production, a 5 percent increase in prices—mean survival. A 2 percent saving on production cost by not putting surplus fertilizer on a field that doesn't need it is significant.

You need to see ahead.

"If you haven't kept records, or can't factor in variables, you are flying blind. You still have to make the basic inputs, change the variables and make the final decision. The computer only makes it easier and faster."

Assuming, you, one of your children and a hired hand have been working 10 fields on which you have records, should you buy or rent? Should you sharecrop or pay cash? Should you hire yourself and your equipment out at custom rates? Should you enter the PIK program? Should you do a little bit of all of these? Should your decision change from year to year and from property to property? If you haven't kept records, or can't factor in variables, you are flying blind. You still have to make the basic inputs, change the variables and make the final decision. The computer only makes it easier and faster.

The purpose of this book is to explain some of the basic terms used in this field and to describe the type of equipment and programs available, the sources of information you can call on and a number of things to avoid. Differing from much of the literature and many of the "consultants," we are *not* tied up with any manufacturer or distributor and can render a somewhat impartial opinion. We have *no* ax to grind.

How to Decide If a Microcomputer Is for You

Opportunities are opening up rapidly in many of the management and operational jobs in U.S. agriculture for an exciting new tool: the microcomputer. Beyond simple bookkeeping jobs, the range of application includes such diverse tasks as calculating the most efficient feed ration in a livestock or poultry enterprise to deciding how much irrigation water is needed in a vineyard or an orchard under any weather forecast.

As this modern technology becomes more price competitive and as improvements are coming at a furious pace, it behooves hundreds of thousands of America's 2.37 million farmers and ranchers to consider a

---

Don't let the cost rule you out.

"There are pros and cons in the case for a computer. But cost is really not one of them. When compared with other agricultural equipment, the cost of a microcomputer system for the farm or ranch is not prohibitive."

---

microcomputer. It might not save them actual working time, because a computer system asks quite a bit in maintenance and care and also because it takes time to master. But in turn, it offers new vistas in helping understand and react to what is actually occurring on the farm or ranch. If a good system is used to its maximum, it could turn around many a struggling agricultural operation. Conversely, there are many other operators, principally those in smaller, less complicated enterprises, whose present methods are working well. They should be especially careful in determining whether a microcomputer would be of real benefit.

There are pros and cons in the case for a computer. But cost is really not one of them. When compared with other agricultural equipment, the cost of a microcomputer system for the farm or ranch is not prohibitive. Numbers will vary widely, but use $5,000 as the ballpark cost of a good, workable system not including software. Still, that's not an insignificant sum even in the big numbers of modern agriculture. Good judgment must be given to such an investment in both your time and your money.

First, as a prospective buyer, you should look at yourself and your current bookkeeping and planning techniques and ask: "What are the jobs that are really important to my success?" Are there, for example, specific financial and operational reasons for buying a microcomputer? Or are there simply personal reasons, such as following the latest trend, or hoping to spend less time in the farm office pushing a pencil?

When you begin to study the possibilities existing in the computer field in that analytical and systematic way, you should quickly begin to identify what kind of information you need, when you need it, how reliable it has to be and how vital it is to obtain it quickly.

Before buying, it also might pay big dividends to capitalize on the experience of others in your agricultural neighborhood who already have computers. Talk to them and ask what they like and dislike about their systems. Find out what they would do differently and then use their experience to prevent your own mistakes in choosing software and a microcomputer system.

It also would be useful to talk to extension agents and officials of the school of agriculture that you already use as resource individuals. They'll be happy to tell you what programs and other public and private resources are available in your area. If you are a purebred livestock or poultry producer, check with your association to learn what systems and software would be compatible with the association's data system. Ask others who already have gone through the experience whether it would be advisable to select software systems before the microcomputer itself. Otherwise you might find you own a microcomputer system that is not compatible with the software programs you will need.

It also will be helpful in reaching a decision on whether to buy, to examine your own business and working habits. Do you enjoy record-keeping and planning, or is that something to be put off until the last minute? A microcomputer probably will not reverse that mind set. But if you really enjoy and take pride in a well-kept set of hand or machine records, and if you like to see a tidy farmstead; neat, straight rows of corn and soybeans; mowed pastures; and farm and office chores done in a systematic way, a microcomputer should add to those pleasures.

Be sure, in essence, you have the mental discipline and temperament to keep regular and detailed records before you take the leap into the age of computers. Otherwise, learning to make the best use of what is essentially an electronic filing and bookkeeping method probably will wind up as a waste of time, money and resources. Before long, it could be catching dust in the corner of the farm office.

However, the odds are that if your office chores require an hour or more a day, you can easily justify a computer. It will be especially handy if that time is spent balancing feed rations at frequent intervals as prices change, planning irrigation schedules, keeping tabs on your purebred livestock herd and poring over other ranch and financial developments.

A computer is only a machine, but it is one that will perform, at very high rates of speed, tasks that might take you hours to complete with a calculator and pencil. It also will give you the ability to hone in on a fine point of management data that you may be already collecting but over-looking in the rush to get other things done.

In spite of its considerable powers, though, a computer system will not correct management or production problems by itself. If you feed it erroneous information, it will process and return invalid conclusions. That, of course, is what has given rise to a cliché in computer circles: "Garbage in, garbage out."

Your ability to make a computer perform like you want it to thus depends on you, the owner-operator. You must learn the required skills and the way to transfer the input correctly to your new system. Its useful-ness lies in the ability to perform literally thousands of mathematical or processing functions in an instant while using information you provide and other data stored in its filing system, or memory bank. To be able to get it to do that will take time. However, requirements are not too forbid-ding. Take typing, for example. Many unskilled typists say they manage the computer keyboard quite nicely with their forefingers, certainly not as fast but adequate for the job.

The main requirement after a suitable system is obtained is a moti-vated learning process. That motivation is the end product of several fac-tors. One is the cost of the system itself. When you decide to invest in a fairly complete system, say, one costing $4,000 to $5,000, you certainly will give it more time and attention than if you purchase one of the low-cost home models, play a few games on it and then let it gather dust.

In that connection motivation equates to time. Putting your system to its highest and best use will take time. The instruction manuals and the software programs that accompany computers are only starting points. At the very least, you will be obligated to learn rudimentary com-puter terminology. Each computer system you will examine will have its own terms. Some systems are "user friendly," meaning they will coincide and track with your own business thought processes. Other programs will lack the quality of friendliness. To make them function, you will have

to learn and understand what will seem to be meaningless instructions on the screen and punch out on the keyboard seemingly illogical commands.

You must have the time to learn.

". . . Motivation equates to time. Putting your system to its highest and best use will take time. The instruction manuals and the software programs that accompany computers are only starting points."

You will not need to become an expert programmer to use a system successfully, though some farmers and ranchers, especially those in specialty crop production or in unique situations, have written their own programs. But, it will be useful to learn a little about programming, just as it would be helpful to know a few phrases of Spanish while visiting in Spain. Writing complete programs for your computer, however, generally is a job for professionals because it is difficult and tedious. Further, generally it is not necessary, because of the variety of off-the-shelf software programs now available in agriculture.

Though the system is just now catching on with producers, the use of computers in agriculture goes back many years. In the 1950's, schools of agriculture in state universities and other operations with large capital budgets, such as extension services, began using big mainframe computers. Those electronic giants, in turn, were used in turning out data received from participating farmers, processed and sent back to them by mail. Such mail-in services were useful in many kinds of record-keeping; however, the turnaround time often was a matter of several days or even weeks.

With agricultural marketing and production developments occurring so rapidly, mail-in records often were outdated and unreliable. So a few progressive farmers found it easier to purchase home computers. Now with the development of microcomputers, that trend is increasing rapidly. Farmers adopting the newer techniques have the advantage of saving much time, wasted effort and money, plus the fact that they can take the cost of a personal computer as a legitimate business expense at tax time.

Agricultural producers with large enterprises obviously have the most to gain from computerization, but smaller farmers and ranchers also are finding they can use computers on a cost-effective basis. The basic point to remember when beginning a search for a compatible system is that it will become a tool to apply modern accounting and record-keeping methods to an agricultural enterprise. It can provide, organize and present information to help make important business decisions.

With the proper software and input, a microcomputer displays information on a screen, showing the operator which decisions will tend to be profitable and which will not. The operator can present the computer with hypothetical data to play the "what if" game. What will happen, for example, if you purchase additional land, what if you add another farrowing house to your hog operation, what if you sell some land and so on.

Using other programs, the microcomputer becomes a tool of communications. Using the proper equipment and software, the operator can tie the computer into large available data sources over telephone lines. The farm computer then can tap into a virtual world of information, including market news, anaylsis and planning programs. Such networks greatly enhance the value and range of computers, bringing into the farm or ranch office data on hundreds of subjects from wire service news reports; stock, livestock and crop quotations; and soil, crop, pest and weather information.

Still another program will give the computer system word-processing capacity. With such a program and other necessary elements, including a printer, you can add professionalism to your business correspondence. During the composing and writing process, you can correct errors before they are transferred to paper. Similarly, you can add, delete or move letters, words, sentences or paragraphs without extensive retyping. You can merge material from two or more files for a new letter or document, assured that a properly programmed technique will flag spelling and grammatical errors. Finally, your printer will turn out a properly spaced and error-free letter once or any number of times.

At the same time, that letter will become a permanent part of your data base management, or electronic, file. Programs for any kind of filing you do in the farm office are relatively inexpensive, and the file capacity is limited only by the data-storage of the computer itself. Most of the new computers have the capacity to accept added memory units for extensive files. That feature is an important point to consider when making the original purchase.

There always will be a nagging doubt in timing the purchase of a computer system. Many would-be purchasers have held back, waiting for new technology or price reductions, or both. Meanwhile they are losing time—and possibly money—in shifting over to the improved systems. A telling point is that if one waits for the ultimate in a small computer system, that time never will come. In a high-technology industry like computers, there always will be something new.

There literally are scores of competitive computer systems on today's market that will meet most agricultural needs for years to come. Though the technology changes, the tasks that a computer performs on the farm or ranch really don't change that much. Technology will improve, of course, but if a computer can help you become more efficient in management today, the money and time you save could be greater than any money saved by waiting.

As a matter of fact, the microcomputer industry is not expected to feature catalog prices that are much lower than those today. The industry already is highly competitive. Additional price reductions in basic equipment probably will be offset by added frills in the equipment of tomorrow. Today's microcomputers and some programs already are more than adequate for most farm and ranch needs.

Far more important for a prospective buyer is the quality of service provided by the manufacturer and vendor. Because most agricultural producers are, by definition, rural, it is important to have your service sources as handily situated as possible. Simply, make sure that your sales source is also a good service and program source. You should not purchase a computer system without a thorough analysis of your needs and

the knowledge that the people with whom you deal know more about computers than merely how to sell them.

Regardless of when you buy a computer system, it should be for the correct reasons. Owning a computer should not be part of a competitive game with friends and neighbors. It should not be a status symbol purchased to keep up with the Joneses. To the contrary, such a purchase should be thought out carefully and based on the jobs you think could be improved upon on the farm or ranch. It also would be a waste of resources to purchase more capacity than you deem necessary for such jobs as record-keeping, enterprise management, market forecasts and quotations, herd management and rations and other statistical jobs. Develop a budget for the computer and receive competitive bids before investing. A good candidate for ownership then will make regular use of the system.

In summary, a computer cannot change a farm or ranch owner's work and professional habits. If those habits are lacking or shoddy going in, so will be the results after computerization. If a candidate, however, has good managerial habits, a new system should enhance the time spent in managing and open up new levels of management and results.

Choosing the Right Support

The conventional wisdom on how to select a computer is that you should buy the software first and then find the hardware to run that software. While that advice often is ignored by the first-time buyer who is completely overwhelmed by the color, size, shape, flashing lights and bells of some new piece of hardware at the local computer store, the "software first, hardware second" dictum is, indeed, a sound one. The question of proper support often is overlooked. For the agricultural buyer, the need for adequate support is so important that the proper order to follow in selecting a computer would be to review support, software and hardware in that order.

The reasoning behind the "software first" logic is based upon the idea that there is, in fact, little difference between the microcomputers on the market today. While they may differ widely in physical appearance and some minor secondary features, their capabilities and construction are basically the same. The microchips that compose the major components of the computer are, in actuality, manufactured by only a handful of companies, yet those microchips are used in all computers on the market today. While more variation exists in the area of *peripheral* devices available for the computer, most companies provide adequate peripheral equipment to enable the agricultural user to accomplish all necessary functions. Further, the microcomputer market now has developed to the point where adequate software can be obtained to perform practically any function desired.

It is not intended that the importance of software selection be relegated to a secondary role, but adequate software is usually available. The availability of adequate support is often a more difficult question. Thus, the quantity and quality of support available may well be the largest variable in structuring a complete computer system.

The support problems facing the agricultural user are not any different from those faced by any microcomputer user. However, certain conditions that usually are present for the agricultural user will tend to compound the effect of support problems. In all probability, the agricultural user will not have a background in computer operation. In addition, agriculture is a unique industry. However, the largest problem facing most agricultural users is one of location.

Seldom situated near a large metropolitan area, the farmer/rancher often will encounter extensive delays in acquiring parts, service, or other forms of support for the newly acquired computer system. Those delays can prove to be both expensive and frustrating. Therefore, the failure to investigate adequately the availability and quality of support services usually will result in disappointment with your new computer system. The assistance you require to install and operate your system, a source of parts and service support may be practically nonexistent in many rural areas. Therefore, you should assure yourself that information support, parts and service are available readily at a reasonable price.

A rural location can be a drawback.

"The assistance you require to install and operate your system, a source of parts and service support may be practically nonexistent in many rural areas. Therefore, you should assure yourself that information support, parts and service are available readily at a reasonable price."

A good place to start your search for support is to insure that the companies which manufacture the hardware and software you intend to purchase and the dealer who sells these products are likely to remain in business. That is not to indicate that only the oldest companies provide satisfactory equipment and support; however, the entire microcomputer industry is in a high state of flux presently, and companies are created and dissolved in matters of weeks and months. Thus, no matter what your contracts say, if the company or dealer is no longer in operation 6 to 12 months after you purchase your equipment, there is little chance that the needed support will be available. The slick brochures and advertising available will do little to inform you about the true status of the company with which you are dealing. A little investigative work on the part of the prospective purchaser to determine the history and reliability of both the dealer and the manufacturer may save untold hours of frustration later. (Figs. 1 and 2)

Probably the first place to start investigating the support available is your point of purchase. That generally will be the place to which you will

return for most of your support. In that regard, there are several types of places where you may be purchasing your computer system. They include a consulting firm, a software store, a computer store or what is termed a turnkey operation.

Generally speaking, the most prevalent and best-known source will be the computer store. Most computer stores specialize in selling hardware with some sales of software packages designed to operate on their particular machines. The software store generally specializes in the selling of software; however, it often recommends the hardware systems on which its software will operate. The turnkey package generally is purchased either at a computer store or at a company specializing in a specific industry, such as agriculture. In the computer industry, the term "turnkey operation" is used to define a situation in which a package of both software and hardware is assembled at one point of sale to meet the purchaser's requirements. If you are working with a consulting firm, it will not sell a specific type of hardware or software. However, it will recommend the type of hardware to be purchased and either write custom software packages or modify existing software packages to meet your specific requirements. While usually the most expensive alternative, a good consulting firm will provide the highest quality of support and service.

Because most purchases will be made through a computer store, that is the area that should be discussed the most. The first, and proba-

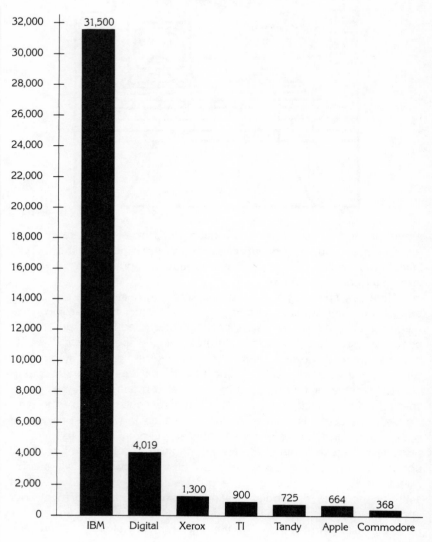

Data Processing Revenue in 1982
(in millions of dollars)

Fig. 1.

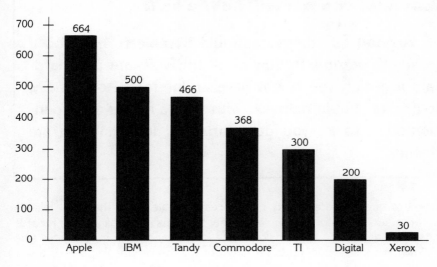

Fig. 2.

bly most important, person with whom you will work in purchasing your computer system is the salesperson. This person must know what is being sold in intricate detail. He or she must understand what you want and work to find it for you. After you buy, the salesperson probably will be the person who will provide you with most of your service and support. If you find yourself in the care of a salesperson who can't do all of this, you could end up with an inadequate system and poor support. One of the first things you should do is ask a few questions of your salesperson to see if you understand each other. There are a lot of specialists who know computers inside and out but couldn't explain them to you if they had to. Some don't even want to. As with all technical personnel, they often find it somewhat self-satisfying to talk above a customer's head. If your salesperson wants mostly to sell you a pet package, find someone else with whom to work. Discover if he or she has a real working knowledge of the store's computer products. A good salesperson should be able to give you a complete demonstration of all the software and hardware in which you might have an interest. Additionally, he or she should help you with a little hands-on experimentation to let you get some feel for what you are buying. If this person can't, find another salesperson or dealer.

Once you have selected a salesperson and a dealer, don't be hesi-

---

Your best contact will be the seller.

"A good salesperson should be able to give you a complete demonstration of all the software and hardware in which you might have an interest. Additionally, he or she should help you with a little hands-on experimentation to let you get some feel for what you are buying."

---

tant to question the quality of services available. Even the most reliable computers occasionally fail. When that happens it means all your records temporarily will be inaccessible. How long they remain inaccessible (the down time) often depends on how quickly the vendor dispatches a service technician and how well prepared the technician is to get your system up and running. Ask about the store's service and support policy. A good dealer will expedite all repairs for you and may be qualified to repair the machine you buy. By exchanging plug-in boards a dealer actually may make repairs while you wait, if you carry your computer into the store. If the vendor offers on-site service, investigate the level of service the maintenance worker is qualified to perform, how far away this person is and how quickly you can expect him or her to be on the scene to repair your broken machine. A good service program should provide a rapid response time, well-qualified technicians and a policy of having the technicians carry a supply of spare parts that will allow them simply to replace ailing circuit boards, thereby reducing the amount of service time. A complete investigation of the service available for your system is important. Computer service is expensive. You should investigate the availability of maintenance contracts, service agreements, extended warranties and any other provisions for service that may be available for the system you select. While a carry-in system of maintenance may be adequate for your particular purposes, it is not recommended that a mail-in or out-of-state service system be considered. The probability of such a maintenance program being satisfactory is extremely remote.

In addition to the basic maintenance of the computer itself, one of the major areas of support that should be investigated is that of publications. The quality of manuals, documentation and other literature available for both software and hardware varies considerably. In the case of hardware, most computers come with a set of technical specification books that will be of great benefit to a repair worker or someone who has to make modifications to your machine. However, these books may be of little value to the user. As a prospective user, you should insure that the machine and the software come with comprehensive, complete and easy-to-understand operating manuals. Prior to purchasing any hardware or software, make sure that you carefully review the manuals to see if you understand them and if they seem to meet your requirements. Again, this is an area where you will want to work closely with your salesperson. Ask him or her to explain the various procedures in the book and show you how those procedures translate to operations on the machine and the software itself. If you find you cannot follow the instructions with your salesperson's help, you may well have a problem when you try to do it without this help. There is nothing more frustrating than trying to utilize your equipment and finding that you cannot follow the instructions contained in the manual, or that the manual does not contain the instructions at all. A complete and comprehensive set of manuals and instruction booklets is among the key features that should be looked for prior to purchasing of equipment or software.

Another area that you may want to consider when contemplating the operational support available to your equipment is the concept of a hotline. That is a relatively new concept whereby certain manufacturers have established a toll-free hotline that enables purchasers of their equipment to call in and ask questions. That is considered to be an excellent support concept, though some users have reported that the quality of the hotline personnel provided by the manufacturers is not as good as they had hoped. It can be anticipated that kind of service will improve in quality as time goes on. With support you have assistance available to you on an every-workday basis that, when used in conjunction with your manual, should enable you to learn to operate your machine in a much more efficient and effective manner. In any event, that type of service should be superior to having to wait and drive to your local computer store to get a question answered.

A careful investigation of the support available for your prospective computer purchase prior to making that purchase will save many hours of frustration after the purchase. Remember that the chain of support generally consists of your salesperson, your dealer, your manufacturer. Your salesperson should be knowledgeable and helpful. If he or she is knowledgeable in both computers and agriculture, it is, indeed, the best of both worlds. Make sure your salesperson can demonstrate completely the hardware he or she is trying to sell, help with your selection of soft-

ware and satisfactorily relate the two to solving your needs. Carefully investigate your dealer's reputation for service and dependability. Have the store personnel been in business long enough to establish a reputation? Will they be in business long enough to service your needs? Do they provide adequate parts support for the system you wish to buy? Do they provide service in the store or at your location? Do they carry a large selection of software that is suitable for your operation? Finally and perhaps most important, what do their current customers have to say about their operation? Does the manufacturer of your prospective purchase provide an adequate quantity of well-written, understandable operating manuals and instructions? Does it provide a toll-free hotline? Is it a large, stable company that will be in business in the foreseeable future? Does it have a good reputation for providing parts and service? If a software manufacturer, does it provide update bulletins as modifications are made to the software package you bought? What warranties are provided by the manufacturer? What additional training programs or self-help materials are made available through the manufacturer to assist you in using your computer? While this list is by no means inclusive, those are some of the areas of support that should be considered prior to making the purchase decision. Those who have overlooked these questions in buying a computer often have lived to regret their oversight.

Selection of the Correct Software

Software is a set of instructions given to a computer to solve a particular problem. That raises two possible problems: The computer has to understand your instructions, and your instructions must be a correct solution to the problem. We will examine the first point by talking about what a computer language is, while the second will involve understanding a flowchart.

Most computers cannot respond to commands given to them in conversational English. In order to communicate with computers, operators must use computer language, or sets of syntax rules, that can be understood by a computer. Some of these computer languages are very similar to English. They are called high-level languages. Low-level languages are more similar to the machine language used by computers. High-level languages are easier for humans to understand but, not surprisingly, take longer to be comprehended by computers. When computers cannot understand the instructions given to them by a programmer, we say that a syntax error has occurred.

Logical errors occur when computers understand the instructions

given to them but the result of their calculations is not a correct answer to the problem. To avoid logical errors, programmers flowchart the solution to a program using certain symbols. Flowcharts describe the flow of information in a program and the different steps necessary to arrive at a solution. They can be a very powerful tool in helping programmers solve problems in the most efficient way.

Although flowcharting symbols (Fig. 3) are fairly uniform among different programmers, there are no standards when it comes to computer languages. BASIC is the language used by about 90 percent of all microcomputers on the market today, but *unfortunately* there exist many different versions of BASIC. Other popular languages include PASCAL, FORTRAN, LOGO and COBOL.

Now that we know what software is, we have to find out how to get it. Your choices are to write your own programs or to buy programs that have been written by somebody else. Most farmers do not have the time to write any but the simplest programs. Programming and particularly debugging (finding errors in a program) can be very time-consuming. Buying written software can be done either by hiring the services of a professional programmer or by purchasing programs from a computer store. Contract programmers can be expensive, and, unless they understand something about farming, and your operation, the results of their work still may not be what you need. They do offer more flexibility, however, than the software packages that you buy at a store.

Software packages are programs with their accompanying documentation, such as manuals and handbooks. Often a particular package is part of a larger collection of programs offered by a software firm. Buying one package from such a collection may allow you to expand the capabilities of your program by an add-on process. PFS Software, for example, sells a line of related PFS software packages such as PFS file, PFS graph, etc. Some products already combine several programs into one. LOTUS 1-2-3, for example, is a package that combines spreadsheet, graphics and data base capabilities.

While software allows the user to give the computer instructions, it also lets the computer communicate with the user. That can be of importance when you are having problems using a program, and you need some help from the computer. User-friendly programs help the user by offering instructions and guidance. User-friendly software makes it easy to learn how to use a program.

There are two other terms used frequently in computer conversations: "ease of learning" and "ease of use." Though the two phrases often are used interchangeably and are somewhat related, they are quite distinct and often opposed in meaning.

FLOWCHART SYMBOLS

Start and Stop

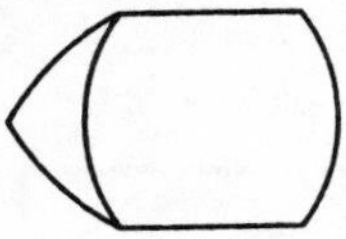

Video Display

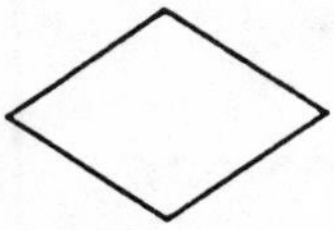

Decision: determine which of a number of alternative paths to follow.

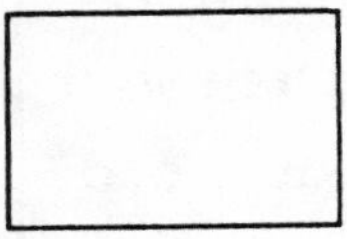

Process or Operation

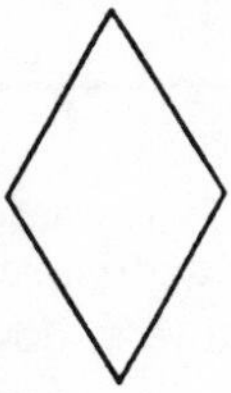

Sort

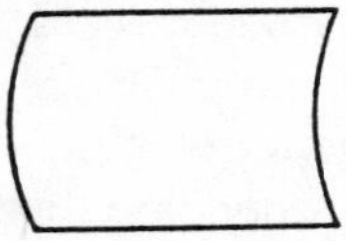

Online Storage

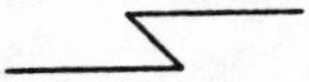

Communication Link

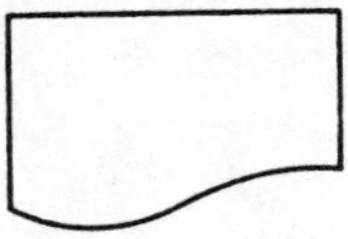

Document: printed output.

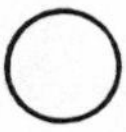

Connector: exit to, or enter from, another part of the flowchart.

Offpage Connector: exit to, or enter from, a page.

Fig. 3.

Ease of learning refers to the simplicity with which a computer novice can develop enough comprehension of the system to complete a simple task. Ease of use refers to a more experienced computer user who can take advantage of the potential power of the system. The factors that make a system easy to learn often are different from those that make it easy to use.

The proper software is the first priority.

"While software allows the user to give the computer instructions, it also lets the computer communicate with the user. That can be of importance when you are having problems using a program, and you need some help from the computer."

If you were to spend every day of your life learning one new program a day, you probably would die of old age before becoming acquainted with every program ever written. This very large volume of software, however, can be divided into some major groups.

Spreadsheets are programs that display columns and rows, or cells, of information on your screen. These cells containing information are then manipulated by the program to give you results in the form of partial totals, combined totals from certain specified cells, etc. Changing the information entered in one cell will result in an automatic recalculation of the totals by the program. The power of electronic spreadsheets resides in their ability to play "what if" scenarios by letting you change the information in a cell and then showing the effect of that cell change on the overall results.

The best spreadsheet programs allow you to go from displaying the data to displaying the formulas by which such data was obtained. For example, if a cell shows an income to your farm of $250 in October, 1983, you also should be allowed to see that that income came from the sale of 100 bushels of corn at $2.50 a bushel. VISICALC is a popular spreadsheet program, but others such as SUPERCALC and MULTIPLAN also exist.

Most of the programs in the record-keeping category have accounting and financial applications. They range from fairly simple programs that help you plan your grocery shopping or balance your checkbook to more complex software that can be used for sophisticated accounting applications. Programs in that category often are used to accomplish such tasks as recording expenses, calculating taxes and figuring depreciation schedules.

Word-processing capability is among the most popular microcomputer programs. This capability enables you to use your micro like a sophisticated typewriter. Word-processing programs let you input text, and then output it in a format that you specify, such as letters or reports. Word-processing programs make it easy to correct from a single word to an entire section of a document, because you can make your corrections by moving the cursor to the desired location on the screen. Some word-processing programs also can help with your spelling, because those programs will bring to your attention words that don't match with a dictionary stored in memory. (Fig. 4)

Other programs (called Data Base Management [DBM]) are a varied group of software. They all attempt to help you organize large amounts of data into categories or files, so that you can manage all this information more effectively. DBM programs can take thousands of numbers, perform mathematical calculations and then output the results with a previously defined format. Although DBM programs are useful to users who have a lot of data and little time to look at it, they also have some limitations. They require large amounts of memory to run, both because they must store much information and because they have to do many things to it. Therefore it is important that you have hardware with sufficient memory to do a good job with DBM programs. Some DBM programs also can be difficult to learn because of their complexity.

More programs are being written for farming and ranching applications. Those include programs for erosion control, fertilizer application, yield estimates, cattle breeding and performance records, ration mixing, commodity trading and hundreds of other applications. Some of those programs may be similar to other software groups described here and could be considered under such categories as well. (Fig. 5)

Several organizations provide both large data bases and software services to microcomputer users via telecommunications networks. Those groups charge a connecting fee to use agricultural information such as USDA reports, weather data and commodity news. Some networks such as The Source, CompuServe, and the Dow Jones News/Retrieval are general information networks that provide data on many

GENERAL SOFTWARE

	Altos	Apple IIe	Atari 800	Com-modore 64	Digital Rainbow	IBM-PC	IBM Data-master	TI Profes-sional	TRS-80 Model 4	Vector Graphic	Victor 9000	Xerox 820	Minimum Memory	Price
SPREADSHEETS														
LOTUS 1-2-3	no	no	no	no	YES[1]	YES	no	YES	no	no	YES[1]	no	128K	$495
MULTIPLAN[2]	no	YES	no	no	YES	YES	no	YES	no	no	no	YES	56K	275
SUPERCALC[2]	YES	YES	no	no	YES	YES	no	YES	YES	YES	no	YES	64K	295
VISICALC	no	YES	YES	no	no	YES	no	no	YES	no	no	no	64K	250
WORD-PROCESSING														
BANK STREET WRITER	no	YES	YES	no	no	no	no	no	no	no	no	no	48K	70
EASY WRITER	no	no	no	no	no	YES	no	no	no	no	no	no	64K	175
PEACH TEXT	YES	YES	no	no	YES	no	no	no	no	YES	no	YES	48K	250
PEACH TEXT 5000	no	no	no	no	no	YES	no	YES	no	no	no	no	128K	395
WORD STAR	no	YES	no	no	no	YES	no	YES	no	no	no	no	64K	495
WORD STAR WITH MAIL MERGE, SPELLING	no	YES	no	no	no	YES	no	YES	no	no	no	no	64K	895

[1]Expected out by first quarter of 1984.
[2]By Microsoft. May require specific operating system.

Fig. 4. This chart lists common software packages and indicates whether or not they will run on a particular computer model.

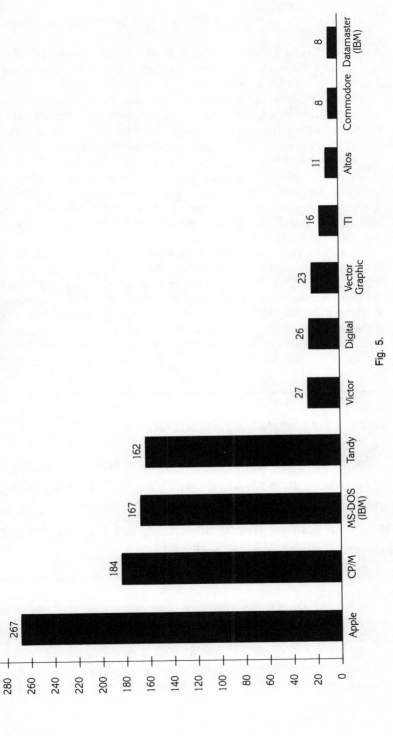

Agricultural Software
(numbers of programs available)

Fig. 5.

topics. But others such as AGNET, AGRISTAR, ProFarmer's Instant Update and Computerized Management Network at Virginia Tech are designed specifically for farming use.

What are some of the important things that make one program better than another? It is not possible to specify a rigid software shopping checklist, because people buy software for many different reasons. Let us review, however, some factors that seem to be of general importance.

It is imperative to identify what you want to do with your programs. Perhaps you want to use your computer solely to play games, or for word-processing. Or maybe you want to accomplish a combination of tasks, such as producing documents given a set of accounting information. In any case, you cannot make an intelligent buying decision until you define your objectives.

How well you define objectives will have a lot to do with the specificity of the program you want. If your objective is general, such as "managing your farm," then the programs you buy necessarily will be rather general. But remember that even if you define a specific objective, such as "record-keeping for 200 dairy cows," the programmers that wrote the software most likely did not know about your particular operation. Becuase no two dairy farms are exactly alike, you need to check carefully that the software does what you are expecting it to do.

Your needs must be identified.

"Perhaps you want to use your computer solely to play games, or for word-processing. Or maybe you want to accomplish a combination of tasks. . . . In any case, you cannot make an intelligent buying decision until you define your objectives."

That brings us to the question, "Can you try the software before you buy it?" It is a very important question, because using a program is really the only way to judge how well you like it. Because software can be copied illegally by unscrupulous users, most software dealers do not accept returns. Some software features preview packages. With these you buy a part of the program at first. If you decide you want the whole program, the manufacturer gives you a release code that unlocks the rest of the program. Of course, if you don't like the program, you must pay for the sample.

Many programs have a demonstration package available at the software dealer store. Those demo programs often run continuously with sample data. They give you a good chance to observe the layout of the program and such features as clarity and limitations. Additionally, some dealers may have an "in store" copy of the program which you may be allowed to use.

Some software manufacturers sell their manuals separately from the software. That will give you a chance to evaluate the program indirectly and will give you a feel for the quality of the documentation. Other sources of information on software include books and magazines which publish software reviews, friends and relatives who have had a chance to try the software, and other farmers and ranchers. Ask the dealer for a list of clients in your area. Then see how the software worked for your colleagues. Keep in mind the concept of specificity discussed earlier, however, since no two farming operations are alike.

The vintage and performance record of the software are also important. Programs that have been out for a while have had a chance to be tested by many users. They are less likely to have errors or "bugs." Ag software that has been tested on the farm or ranch has a definite advantage over an untested program. There is generally nothing wrong, how-

ever, with buying a recently updated release of a well-tested program because it is likely to incorporate the changes and suggestions introduced by previous users.

Because software constantly is updated, you should investigate what software maintenance the dealer is offering. What if you find an error in your program? Will the manufacturer charge to have your program changed or updated? Asking these important questions and keeping these general concepts in mind will help in making the decision that is right for your farm or ranch.

Hardware Selection Is
Your Next Step

Before talking about the physical devices of a microcomputer system, or hardware, we need to define another component of a computer system: the operating system. The operating system of a computer is an intermediate step between the software and hardware. (Fig. 6) It is a set of instructions, or a program, that coordinates the operations of a computer. The operating system performs many tasks such as testing the condition of the hardware upon power-on, searching for data in storage devices and operating the monitor and printer. By providing this set of "game rules" to the computer, it eliminates the need for having such

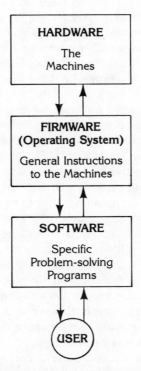

Fig. 6. The relationship between hardware, firmware, software and the user in a computer system.

instructions attached to each software program, thus increasing the effi-
ciency of the computer system.

The operating system and software differ in their relationship with
hardware. The operating system is associated much more closely with a
physical device than is software. The IBM Disk Operating System would
be considered an operating system because it is designed specifically for
controlling the operation of the IBM Personal Computer.

As you may have realized already, the difference between the operating system and software is not a sharp one. There is no one standard
operating system. Operating system packages such as CP/M, MP/M,
UNIX and MS-DOS, for example, have been designed to operate on
more than one hardware system. These generally are referred to as
generic operating systems. Operating systems such as Appledos, Trsdos
and Hdos can be used only on one type of computer and are known as
proprietary operating systems.

The practical significance of this is that a generic operating system
makes it easier to use the same software on different machines. When
thinking about what hardware to buy, looking at what operating system is
used to run the computer will give you an idea of how easy it may be for
you to use your programs on other computers, or to exchange files with
users of other systems. Operating systems differ from one another in
speed of operating and in degree of "friendliness" (the amount of on-
screen help they provide a user).

A further distinction appears when we examine how many jobs an
operating system package can handle at one time. Most personal computers use packages that are single-thread operating systems. These systems can handle only one job at a time. But other computers use multi-
tasking operating systems that can do more than one job simultaneously.
For example, multi-tasking systems will allow you to work on updating a
financial report while the computer's printer is typing a letter.

Although it is beyond the scope of this book to recommend a specific operating system package, you should be aware that selecting a
microcomputer that uses little-known operating systems may restrict
your choice of software. Your computer must have an operating system
which is compatible with the applications programs you want to run.
Many computer manufacturers today are allowing their systems to be run
under generic operating systems if the user so desires. Choosing a computer that accepts a well-known generic operating system such as CP/M
or MS-DOS is probably a wise decision.

Hardware is that part of a computer system you can put your hands
on, something you can touch and see. Because hardware is generally the
most expensive component of a computer system, you need to consider

---

Hardware is the system's heart.

"Hardware is that part of a computer system you can put your hands on, something you can touch and see. Because hardware is generally the most expensive component of a computer system, you need to consider carefully what hardware you need. . . ."

---

carefully what hardware you need and to get acquainted with some elementary concepts about computer hardware.

The various parts that compose a typical microcomputer system are shown in Fig. 7. Refer to this figure often as you read this chapter so that you can visualize the various hardware components.

The Central Processing Unit (CPU) is the heart of the computer. The CPU executes complex tasks by using a microprocessor. A microprocessor is a miniaturized electronic circuit that contains complete computer-processing logic, often in a space 1 by ½ inch or less. Information travels in the microprocessor in definite quantities called bytes. Each byte is composed of eight bits, and each bit is either a 0 or a 1. So a byte is just a certain amount of information that is recognized by the microprocessor for its particular combination of eight 0's and 1's. Because computers can handle a large amount of bytes, most people talk of computer capabilities in terms of kbytes (or K), where one kbyte equals about 1,000 bytes.

The CPU contains the microprocessor and other electronic circuits within a framework that is often referred to as the "Mother Board." Additional electronic circuits or boards can be plugged into this mother board to increase the processing power of the microcomputer. Most micros, for example, will accept an additional graphics board to improve graphics quality.

In order for the CPU to obtain data to work on, or to save the results of its operations, a certain amount of memory is required. Computer memory is also quantified in terms of bytes and kbytes. There are two types of memory: read only memory (ROM) and random access memory (RAM). ROM is a small amount of memory (4K in the Apple III, for example) that is used to perform internal computer functions. These

PARTS OF A COMPUTER SYSTEM

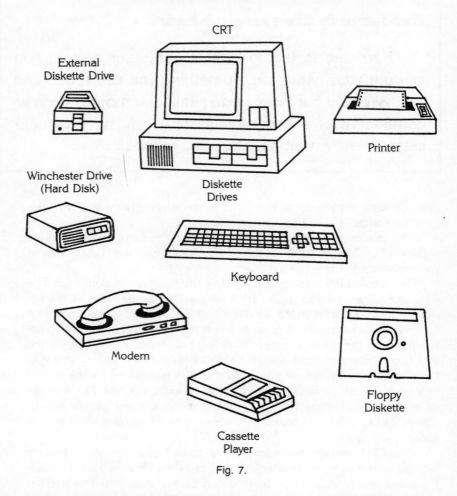

Fig. 7.

internal functions are controlled by programs that permanently reside in ROM. These programs are called "firmware." Of far greater importance to the user is the amount of RAM available, because this is the memory used by the computer to run programs.

When power to the computer is switched off, everything in the RAM is lost, and only the information in ROM is saved. To prevent the information in RAM from being lost, it is necessary for the computer to have permanent storage devices. There are three types of commonly used storage devices: cassette tapes, floppy disks (also called diskettes) and hard disks. Cassette tapes are the cheapest, but also the slowest and least reliable storage medium. Floppy disks are flexible disks 5¼ or 8 inches in diameter on which information is stored magnetically. They are the most commonly used storage device. Hard disks can store large amounts of information but are also very expensive. Both floppy and hard disks are operated by disk drives, which rotate the disks to search for information.

A computer must be able to communicate with the user. A keyboard is commonly used to enter instructions or data into the computer. Keyboards can be as simple as a plastic membrane with the characters printed on it, or as sophisticated as a typewriter keyboard with program-mable keys. Membrane keyboards are adequate to accomplish simple programming tasks. For chores such as word-processing which require fast typing you need a typewriter keyboard. Programmable keys that can replace many keystrokes with one are features of some keyboards. Two other important features to look for when selecting a computer are a numeric keypad and a detachable keyboard. A numeric keypad is a square of keys to the right of the regular keyboard, arranged like an adding machine, that allows you to enter numbers quickly and easily. A detachable keyboard allows you to place the video screen where it's most comfortable for viewing, and the keyboard where it's most comfortable for typing. If the keyboard and video display are all in one piece, your options for shifting positions are limited.

Montoring the computer's operations is usually done with the use of a video display terminal (VDT), also known as a cathode ray tube (CRT) or simply a monitor. Some computers do not come with a monitor. You have to use your TV set to see the results of your work. Monitors can be either monochrome (one color) or color, with the former being adequate for most agribusiness applications. Most planning and financial pro-grams often used on the farm require monitors that can display at least 40 and preferably 80 columns of text.

To get the results of the computer's work on paper, you must use a printer. Printers can be classified in two major groups: dot-matrix and letter-quality. Dot-matrix printers form a character by driving a set of closely spaced wires or pins against an inked ribbon. They can print at a very high speed for fast work (160 characters per second) and at a rela-tively slow speed (40 characters per second) for better print quality. This high-quality printing is achieved by double-striking, having a print head make several passes over a print line with the head position offset slightly on each pass. These printers are relatively inexpensive and are well suited to printing graphics.

Letter-quality printers provide excellent print quality at moderately fast print speed, 10 to 45 characters per second. Several kinds of letter-quality printers exist, including daisy wheel printers which feature individual letters on the spokes of a rotating disk, and thimble printers which have a thimble-shaped print element that spins during operation. Both of these types of letter-quality printers usually feature changeable print elements that allow the use of different type fonts. (Fig. 8)

PRINTERS[1]

Type	Brand	Speed (CPS)[2]	Maximum Paper Width (Inches)	Price (Dollars)
Dot-Matrix	Microline 82A	120	8½	549
	Mannesman Tally MT160L	160/40[3]	10	798
	Epson FX 100	160/80[3]	16	999
Daisy Wheel	Brother HR 25	24	15½	895
	Diablo 630	40	15½	2495

[1]Each printer manufacturer may offer several models.
[2]CPS—Characters per second.
[3]Two-speed printer.

Fig. 8.

Modems (modulator-demodulator devices) allow you to communicate with other computers, generally by using phone lines. The speed at which modems communicate is gauged in terms of bauds, with a baud equalling one bit per second. Although some computers communicate at the relatively low speed of 300 baud, most microcomputer modems operate at 1,200 baud. Modems allow microcomputer owners to use ag-information networks and financial and commodities news services. Many computer information networks can be accessed with a modem, allowing you to do things that range from posting a "For Sale" ad on an electronic bulletin board to making your own flight reservations.

When dealing with a technical subject that is changing as rapidly as microcomputers are, any type classification should be considered tentative at best. To help you make sense of the large microcomputer market,

however, we suggest that it be divided into desktop and portable micro-computers.

Desktop microcomputers are not designed to be frequently and readily moved, or to be taken on a business trip. Desktop microcomputers can be divided further into home, personal, and business or advanced systems.

Home computers are also often called "recreational" or "game" computers. They are inexpensive (generally less than $500) and simple systems that can be connected to your TV. They generally emphasize recreational and educational applications. They are ideal for learning about computers but have limited application to farm management. Examples in this category include the Timex-Sinclair 1000, TRS-80 Color Computer, TI-99/4A, Commodore Vic 20 and Atari 400.

Personal (or general-purpose) microcomputers are the group that people identify most readily as the "typical" microcomputers. Equipped with 32K to 128K of RAM and costing from about $1,000 to $5,000, they can run many ag-software programs while also performing other tasks such as word-processing and financial forecasting. Examples include the Apple II series, TRS 80 Models III and IV, IBM PC, Commodore 64 and Atari 800.

Business or advanced microcomputers are sophisticated systems with at least 128K RAM, costing $7,000 and up. Although they have the capacity of running complex software, their price may put them beyond the reach of most farm-oriented users. Certain microcomputer systems such as the IBM Datamaster System/23 are not to be confused with personal computers, as they can handle much larger amounts of data and the cost of an installed system may approach $15,000.

In contrast to desktop microcomputers, portable microcomputers feature some ease of mobility. They often are subdivided into transportable microcomputers, which require a fair amount of effort to be moved, "true" portable micros that can be moved around by one person, and pocket micros that may weigh as little as 4 ounces. Although they have some restrictions, such as reduced monitor size, portable micros can be helpful as quick, on-the-farm decision-making tools.

Microcomputers can also be classified by the length of their instruction or data word. The two most common lengths are 8-bit and 16-bit. An individual 16-bit instruction is more than twice as powerful as an 8-bit instruction, and programs run faster. Also, a 16-bit computer can have more user-programmable memory. Often the maximum memory on a 8-bit computer is 64K, while on a 16-bit computer the maximum may exceed 512K. Some computer vendors have found ways to stretch 8-bit computers to 128K. The 8-bit computers have been in production much longer than 16-bit machines. Therefore there are considerably more software packages available for 8-bit processors. The most popular operating system, CP/M, runs on an 8-bit Z80 chip. Many programs available for the 16-bit machines were once 8-bit programs that were quickly rewritten to run on the 16-bit computers. To take advantage of all the 8-bit programs, some 16-bit computers (such as Vector 4 and DEC Rainbow) contain a second processor that is 8 bits. The dual-processor system will run programs written for CP/M and the 16-bit CP/M-86 operating system.

There are hundreds of different brands and models of microcomputers, but not all of them are able to run ag software. The Apple II and Radio Shack TRS 80 Model III and IV series are the two microcomputer systems that presently have the largest number of ag software programs written for them. That means that microcomputers that are software-compatible with these systems (such as the Apple III and the various Radio Shack TRS 80 micros) may also run the same software.

Each of the latest models in these two series (the Apple IIe and the TRS 80 Model IV) have 64K RAM, with two disk drives, an 80-column monitor and a dot-matrix printer. You can expect to pay about $2,900 for either system.

A large number of programs has been written for use with CP/M, a generic firmware package. As a result of this, many computers that run their own software also run CP/M programs. They include the Apple II, TRS 80, Vector 4, Commodore 64 and, shortly, the Atari 800.

The IBM PC costs about $4,000 for a 64K RAM model with two disk drives, an 80-column monitor and a dot-matrix printer. For about $700, you can buy a board (Quadram Quadlink) that plugs into the PC and lets you run about 90 percent of Apple software.

One consideration is paramount.

"Through your whole [buying] process, however, you should always keep in mind the most important question to ask when buying a microcomputer: Is this system going to do what I want?"

There are other microcomputers that can run ag software, and as time passes, more programs are likely to be written for each different model. But how do you go about choosing the right system? (Fig. 9)

Some of the important steps to choosing the right hardware are outlined below. Through your whole decision process, however, you should always keep in mind the most important question to ask when buying a microcomputer: Is this system going to do what I want?

a. Defining your objectives: What do you want your computer to do? If you are interested in games, for example, good color graphics and sound are important considerations. For word-processing, on the other hand, a screen that is easy on the eyes, an 80-column monitor and a good keyboard are musts.

b. Software availability: Because development often lags two to three years behind hardware, it is crucial that the hardware you buy can run the programs that you want.

c. Memory requirements: Once you have decided what programs you want to run, check that your hardware has the memory required to do the job. Most software packages have a specified minimum amount of RAM needed for successful execution.

d. Expansion: It is better to buy a simple system that can be expanded than to have to sell your first system for a more powerful one. Make sure that your hardware (generally the CPU) has expansion slots to add items such as additional disk drives or printers.

e. Documentation and support: Make sure that the hardware you are buying has a clear owner's manual, good instructions on maintenance and an address to write to and a phone number to call should you have any questions about your system.

f. Warranty: Be sure to understand and read the warranty specifications of your system. Ask the dealer how long it takes to get something fixed by the manufacturer.

g. Tax considerations: Remember that hardware costs can be deducted from your taxes as a regular business expense. Investment tax credits also are available for hardware purchases. You should consult with your tax accountant on the specific details.

Fig. 9 offers a comparison of certain features for several computer models currently available. Here is a brief explanation of the categories:

Word Size

There are basically two types of microprocessors in personal computers: 8-bit and 16-bit. The 16-bit microprocessors are more powerful than the 8-bit. A limited number of machines have both 8-bit and 16-bit.

BRAND	Word Size (Bits)	Maximum Memory	Minimum Storage 2 Diskette Drives	Maximum Storage 2 Diskette Drives	Hard Disk	Special Function Key	Numeric Keypad	Modem	Operating Systems	Price
ALTOS SERIES 5-15	8	192K[1]	2000K	2000K	YES	YES	YES	YES	CP/M, MP/M-86	$4000
APPLE IIe	8	128K	280K	280K	YES	no	no	YES	DOS, 3.3, CP/M, UCSD-P	2565
ATARI 800	8	48K	176K	176K	no	no	no	YES	DOS I or II	1600
COMMODORE 64[2]	8	64K	340K	340K	YES	YES	no	YES	DOS, CP/M	830
DIGITAL RAINBOW 100	8/16[3]	256K	800K	800K	YES	YES	YES	YES	CP/M-86/80, MS-DOS	3715
IBM PC	16	640K	360K	720K	YES	YES	YES	YES	CP/M-86, MS-DOS, UCSD-P	3400
IBM DATAMASTER	8	128K[4]	2200K	2200K	YES	YES	YES	YES	IBM	7040
TI PROFESSIONAL COMPUTER	16	256K	640K	640K	YES	YES	YES	YES	CP/M-86, MS-DOS, UCSD-P	2710
TRS-80 Model 4	8	128K	360K	360K	YES	YES	YES	YES	TRSDOS, CP/M, L-DOS	1999
VECTOR GRAPHIC	8/16[3]	256K[4]	630K	630K	YES	YES	YES	YES	CP/M, CP/M-86, MS-DOS	3995
VICTOR 9000	16	896K[4]	1200K	2400K	YES	YES	YES	YES	CP/M-86, MS-DOS	3495
XEROX 820-II	8	64K	310K	624K	YES	no	YES	YES	CP/M	2595

[1]192K minimum.
[2]CRT has 40-column display.
[3]Dual processors.
[4]128K minimum.

Fig. 9.

Maximum Memory

Maximum memory is the total amount of RAM memory available through expansion. This is an important consideration if you plan to enlarge your computer operations. Software programs require different amounts of memory capacity. Memory is expressed in K, or kilobytes (1,024 bits).

Minimum and Maximum Diskette Storage

These minimums and maximums are given only as a guide for a typical two-diskette drive system. It is possible to buy a system with no diskette drives or up to four diskette drives. This depends on the computer system and the user's needs. Diskette drives come in two formats: those that read single-sided diskettes and those that read double-sided diskettes. Some computer systems use double-density diskettes. This is a way of storing information on diskette that increases the capacity to twice that of a standard diskette. The amount of information that can be stored on a diskette is also expressed in K.

Hard Disk

The availability of hard disk, a high-capacity magnetic storage medium, is a means of expansion to a computer system.

Special Function Key

These special keys are used in some software packages to simplify certain operations. They allow you to press one key instead of a series of two or three.

Numeric Keypad

A square of keys to the right of the keyboard allows you to enter numbers quickly. They keys are arranged like an adding machine. This is an important feature to look for if you will be entering numeric data frequently.

Modem

That is the hardware that enables a computer system to communicate with other systems via telephone lines. A modem is a must if you intend to tie into networks now or in the future. Additional software is also needed, but it is important that the computer you buy have the ability to add a modem.

Operating Systems

The operating system determines the software programs that can be run on a computer. Some computers use a system developed specifically for that model, while others use operating systems such as CP/M that can be run on a variety of computers. Though some operating systems can be run on different computers, there still may be a problem. Almost every manufacturer of personal computers has its own format for storing information on diskette. Even if a program were written onto a diskette using the CP/M operating system, it would probably not be compatible with any other computer, even if that computer were designed to run CP/M. Downloading is a way of transferring information on diskette from one machine format to another. This can be done by some software dealers or computer stores.

Price

These are not list prices. They were quoted by various computer stores for a basic system designed to meet the needs of the typical user. Each prospective buyer will select a system tailored to his or her particular situation. The basic system represented here features 64K memory; a keyboard; monochrome CRT (or video monitor) with 80-column format; two-disk drives of minimum size; the basic operating system, if any, that comes with the model; and the ability to add a printer. The prices listed do not include the cost of a printer itself. It is likely that the user will want to add a 132-character, good-quality printer, which will increase the price of the system by $500 or so.

Your Computer Will Need a Good Home

As an agricultural producer, you already know how important it is to provide a good environment for your crops and livestock. No matter how hard you try, you simply cannot grow 100-bushel corn on land more suited to pasture. Though your new microcomputer system is only a sophisticated assembly of machinery and electronics, it, too, requires a carefully controlled environment to perform properly.

Perhaps more care must be given a computer than any other machinery. Dirt, in the form of dust or any other contamination, is the mortal enemy of the computer.

Before you make a final choice on a computer system, there are a minimum of seven factors that deserve careful consideration. They are: office space, maintenance of the system, proximity to an electrical power source and the quality of that source, proximity to a telephone system, operating and support supplies, quality and extent of backup support and insurance coverage.

None of those—and possibly others that might come into play in special situations—can be taken lightly. Inadequate follow-through can lead only to serious inconvenience at a time you can afford it least.

Even in the normal home-office atmosphere, your computer should be cleaned completely at least once a month. For best results follow the instructions in your owner's manual.

Diskettes are designed to store information for long periods of time, but this information may be lost if the diskette is not properly cared for. Here are some important care considerations.

- Always keep diskettes in their envelopes when you are not using them. A diskette is damaged by contamination when the recording surface is touched, spotted or dampened by an oily, sticky or abrasive substance.
- A similar problem may arise if the diskette is bent. Don't force your diskette in or out of drives. To avoid warping, store diskettes flat in their envelopes in stacks of 10 or less, or vertically, supporting them so they do not lean or sag.
- Do not apply pressure to the diskette. Write on labels before applying them to the diskette, or use a felt-tip marker to write on labels that already are attached.

— Sunlight and temperature extremes can warp your diskette. Other environmental factors such as magnetic fields and electronic currents can erase information from the surface of the diskette. Be careful not to store diskettes too close to the telephone or carry them through airport security with magnetic detection devices.
— A special diskette can be purchased to clean the disk head on your computer. It should be used on a regular basis to remove any particles that might build up.

However, today's microcomputers are not nearly as finicky as the first-generation mainframe computers were a few years ago. Consider: Then most computers were housed in special glass-walled rooms, where temperature and humidity could be controlled to a precise degree, where air was filtered and where smoking, drinking and eating were prohibited. To work with them required a degree of cleanliness more suited to the operating room of a hospital than a commercial workplace. In large corporations using the large computers, you may still find glass rooms walled off from the rest of the building.

When microcomputers arrived on the scene, they began moving into open, uncontrolled spaces in home and professional offices, in stores, out in factories and, yes, in agricultural production enterprises. That brought with them a corresponding increase in problems resulting from dirt, dust and other contaminations, including excess heat, humidity and so on. Most manufacturers of microcomputers recognized the problem and incorporated within the framework of their products various shields, insulations and filtering equipment. Still, dirt of various kinds is a problem for microcomputers because there are no totally clean farm offices or homes.

Computers like the clean life.

". . . Dust and dirt are only one face of contamination. Extreme heat and cold are others. Heat is a particularly sneaky villain. By the same token, if the system becomes too cold, some of the mechanical functions like disk accesses and printing can become sluggish."

Even the computer itself must take part of the blame. Contamination can result from particles of printer paper, oxide from tapes and disks, fibers broken loose from printer ribbons and so on.

For agricultural use in particular, one type of contamination to consider is the use of auxiliary heating units, such as kerosene heaters or wood stoves. Even the most efficient kerosene heaters give off a mist, which can condense on circuit boards, chips, disks and so on, where it can do immeasurable damage. In the same area, wood, oil or coal stoves are simply too dirty to use near a computer that is allergic to ash, smoke and coal dust.

But dust and dirt are only one face of contamination. Extreme heat and cold are others. Heat is a particularly sneaky villain. By the same token, if the system becomes too cold, some of the mechanical functions like disk accesses and printing can become sluggish.

The mere fact of adding functions to your computing system may cause temperature problems. With smaller machines the situation can worsen when auxiliary equipment is stacked atop earlier units. Placing the monitor screen above the disk drive, for example, could block the cooling of lower units.

In planning your installation now and in the future, no system ever should be damaged by heat. If you keep equipment away from the sources of direct heat and out of direct sunlight, that should solve most of the problems. In addition, keep equipment clean, allow sufficient space for free air flow, don't stack components vertically, and provide for additional cooling when possible.

Another kind of contamination that falls into a separate category is the possibility of magnetic or electromagnetic fields. They can be damaging to the system by disrupting the system's operations directly, by altering data and by erasing magnetic storage, or memory, functions. All kinds of motors, bells, buzzers, transformers and other electric and mechanical equipment either have some kind of permanent magnetic devices or generate electromagnetic current. Even an innocent-appearing pliers or wrench could be magnetized, as could something else in your office, like scissors, staples or paper clips.

The bell of the ordinary telephone, your audio speaker, an office radio or a CB unit can be a troublesome offender.

Such stray and random hazards, which can be difficult to find, transform themselves into foes of your disk drives, memory bank or other units. The result may be garbled data, false printouts or other unexpected breaks in the smooth operation of the system.

Again, as in temperature and humidity extremes, such problems can be solved rather easily, once they are identified. Simply by moving the offenders out of range, possibly 3 to 6 feet away, the problem is corrected. Or, if a unit cannot be moved physically, it may be possible to shield it from the computer by using a thin sheet of carbon steel or iron.

Another computer hazard may be static electricity, which could pose a serious problem for malfunctioning of the system. That rarely happens. Floor surfaces of any kind are troublesome; in particular, wall-to-wall carpeting. Static thus generated can alter or wipe out the contents of a computer's memory, generate faulty data, blank out a video display or create a host of other relatively serious problems.

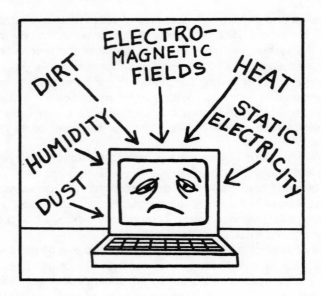

The potential for trouble can be reduced by proper grounding of all computer electric lines. The service of a qualified electrician is vital to see that this is done. Other steps include the removal of offending carpets, including some kinds of vinyl tiling, and not wearing crepe- or rubber-soled shoes while working on the system. There also are available anti-static mats to be used under the computer cabinets, desks or chairs.

The list of problems goes on and on. It behooves the new system owner-operator to be aware of them as places to investigate if the computer system does not operate as it should.

Electric power disturbances, especially in rural areas, can be a major problem in malfunctioning. Even in cases in which power does not go completely off, other things like low voltage, surges, line noise and other operating mishaps can cause havoc with program and computer memory loss and other computer operations. There is also a worse danger in that such discharges can burn out circuit chips or entire circuit boards.

The worst part of that possibility is the fact that the farm or ranch owner-operator cannot do much about prevention of electric transmission problems. About all the farmer or rancher can do is to buy and install appropriate devices, including standby power sources. Some of the preventive measures require substantial investments in remedial equipment; others cost less. The new owner will have to decide how much protection is needed, but in making the transition to a computer system he or she should be aware of the potential for trouble, especially in areas in which power disruptions are fairly frequent.

Those are some of the problems that can be expected; there are others. The most important point to remember is that the cause of the problem and its correction tend to be obvious with a little experience. You can overcome most of the possibilities with advance care, such as taking care of dirt and contamination problems, magnetic fields, static charges, power disturbances and so on. By doing those tasks on a routine basis, you also can prolong the working life of the computer itself and other mechanical and electronic components of the system.

As you buy and install the computer and the auxiliary equipment you need, there are other considerations to keep in mind. Most equipment is designed to operate on 110 volts, but there is some requiring 220 volts. When plugging in a new system, the new operator should check

the home or farm office circuit system and be sure to use either a new circuit or one that has the lowest level of use. If your computer, for example, winds up on a circuit that already is being used for adding machines, electric typewriters and so on, problems could be encountered. The contents of the computer's memory system simply could disappear if someone else decided to switch on an electric typewriter on an overloaded circuit, or if another piece of electrical equipment switched on at an inopportune time.

Ideally, your new computer system should be the only appliance drawing power from that particular circuit. If that is not possible, be sure it is not on a circuit with other appliances like air conditioners, freezers or refrigerators.

To expand its horizons and usefulness dramatically, you should arrange for your new computer system to have direct access to a business telephone, something that even in this day may not be easy to do in certain areas of the United States. With the purchase of a modem, a piece of equipment that ties your computer into a telephone system, the possibilities for use are limited only by the number of services to which you subscribe.

With a modem, the farm or ranch microcomputer can be used as what is called a "smart terminal" with access to computer programs from various universities, news, livestock and crop price quotations, stock market information and other commercial time-sharing services.

Such dial-up facilities are available from scores of schools of agriculture, farm organizations and other agriculturally oriented groups. Balanced livestock ration programs, pest management control problems, irrigation and fertilization schedules, marketing information and weather forecasts are only a few examples of available programs that are beyond the scope of most home microcomputer programs because they must be updated daily, even hourly, to be useful.

However, those providing those services keep their programs timely. Subscribers can tap into any one of them at any time for the price of a telephone call, plus the subscription price of the service. If an agricultural computer system is utilized as it should be to justify its time and expense, the additional purchase and use of a modem is essential.

Not a lot can be said about a backup system or supplies for your new farm or ranch microcomputer because each user's needs will vary widely. Those problems should be considered on an individual basis. However, backing up data and programs is vital. How much printer paper you need to keep in stock, for example, will depend on how many printouts you will be generating, or how much correspondence will result from your word-processing activity. Similarly, can your enterprise afford to be without its microcomputer for a week or two, while repairs are being made, or does it need immediate and ongoing backup? In a purebred livestock operation, surely registrations or other herd information can be postponed briefly, but irrigation information for that wilting crop may be vital on a daily basis.

Don't forget insurance coverage.

"Any mishap or damage to the computer equipment, its modem facility or other environmental housing can be costly as well as having a disastrous impact on the full farm or ranch operation. To insure against such losses is prudent."

At least one other environmental consideration for your microcomputer is a must. That is insurance coverage.

Any mishap or damage to the computer equipment, its modem facility or other environmental housing can be costly as well as having a disastrous impact on the full farm or ranch operation. To insure against such losses is prudent. The problem may be that the owner-operator is into a new field, and so are the agents from whom coverage is purchased.

Insurance on leased equipment, for example, is a very complex area, but here we are assuming that the farmer or rancher will purchase the system. It cannot be overemphasized that customary forms of equipment coverage do not provide protection in the area of data processing, which is what microcomputers basically are. There are specialized policies, however, that insure against all risks of physical loss or damage to such equipment and do not exclude losses from acts of God or unexplained or mysterious disappearances. It is possible to insure against the loss of a computer program on a disk drive or an electronic tape, even when the disk or tape seemingly is on hand and intact. But the new owner should be extremely careful that both he or she and the insurer understand and take into account such a problem when the policy is being issued.

It may be that the most advantageous way would be to purchase an all-inclusive records insurance policy, including all valuable papers and records as well as the data processing media. The computer system also should be insured against a business interruption brought about by some failure or mishap and possibly should be covered by extra expense insurance, if the computer functions must be carried on manually after a failure.

In brief, the providing of adequate insurance for a newly installed microcomputer system on the farm or ranch is complex and likely to be a completely new business for both the prospective policy holder and writer. As it should be at any time, it will be critical for the insurance buyer to read and understand the fine print.

Are you asking yourself by now whether you really need a computer system in the light of all that goes with it? For some prospective purchasers a review of the buying decision will be in order. Maybe hand record-keeping is not so cumbersome after all. However, computers truly are the way of the future. If prudently managed and maintained, an agricultural computing system should pay enormous dividends to all those producers who own and manage commercial enterprises.

New Owners Should Be Educated

Plowing a field, calibrating a planter, operating a grain combine—these are all operations that require a high degree of skill and training. Although practice is by far the most important way to learn how to do these chores, proper instruction at the right time can save you a lot of work. A similar situation exists with microcomputers. The best way to learn to use them is practice, but receiving the proper education can help. There are several alternatives available for those who are seeking computer instruction.

Because the average microcomputer buyer probably is not willing to spend the next four years of his or her life in college, we won't talk here about full-time educational opportunities. Most major universities in the U.S., and particularly land-grant colleges, offer continuing education courses (CEC's) in computer science. These CEC's typically cost less than $300 for tuition, last from 1 to 15 weeks (averaging about 4) and often are taught in the evenings or on weekends. While some courses are general introductions for beginners, others offer advanced training in complex programming techniques.

Private institutions, including colleges, technical schools and even computer manufacturers and dealers, also offer courses. Manufacturers of hardware found that it is cheaper to train people to use their products correctly than to keep a large maintenance and repair staff, so they often offer courses at reasonable rates.

If you are not sure of whether a microcomputer is what you need, or even if you are just interested in getting some general knowledge about micros, general introductory courses are an excellent choice. Some people tend to worry too much about learning the specific details of a programming language without first getting a good idea of some general problem-solving concepts. Once you have learned how to cope with computers, getting acquainted with a specific system will be much easier. Learning a computer language predisposes your mind to think somewhat in parallel to how a computer thinks, and makes learning other languages much easier. Of course, some people don't have the time to do so, and there is nothing wrong with going directly to what interests you.

Further advantages of taking a computer course at a learning institution include the access to qualified tutors, such as professional programmers, who can help with your questions, and the chance to use the institution's hardware. Although you will not be allowed to test the sturdiness of a particular microcomputer system by tossing it out of the classroom window, a computer course gives you an excellent chance to test the capabilities of a system. Most instructors, in fact, will make comments about the advantages or disadvantages of a particular piece of hardware or software. Additionally, because the data you will be using probably is not going to be of importance to you, you will be able to experiment at your leisure with the system without having to worry about mistakes.

Ask your neighbors how to do it.

"There are many sources of computer knowledge that do not require great commitments of money and time. Friends and relatives who own or are experienced with microcomputers are excellent sources of information. It generally is easier to ask them . . . than to deal with strangers."

There are many sources of computer knowledge that do not require great commitments of money and time. Friends and relatives who own or are experienced with microcomputers are excellent sources of information. It is generally easier to ask them about a system than to deal with strangers. Similarly, neighboring farmers or ranchers can give you a good idea on how their microcomputers have performed in their operations. If possible, ask what specific advantages or problems they have found, and then keep in mind the differences between your farm operation and theirs.

User groups are formed by owners of a particular microcomputer system and often can be contacted by checking ads in magazines or in computer networks such as The Source and CompuServe. Also, most computer stores either have a bulletin board area where users can post notices or are willing to give you a users' list so that you can get in touch with other computer owners. User groups offer excellent opportunities to share problems and discoveries with persons who own hardware similar to yours. Although at the beginning you may be overwhelmed by the technical jargon (or "computerese") spoken by computer buffs, you soon will pick it up yourself and feel a lot more comfortable when dealing with others.

State agricultural extension offices organize computer seminars and workshops targeted specifically to farm users. These workshops last from one-half day to two days and give farmers a chance to try different models of microcomputers and various ag software programs. Most extension services offer seminars on a rotational basis in different parts of the state, so try to attend a workshop that is scheduled in your area. They usually are timed to coincide with a period of the year when farm activities are at a low point (such as after harvest) and generally cost about $50. Private farm organizations such as the Professional Farmers of America also offer excellent computer workshops, but be prepared to spend higher registration fees (about $200).

Before attending a seminar or workshop, be sure it is the one that is right for you. Not all computer workshops concentrate on farming applications. You could find yourself sitting among lawyers or bankers rather than farmers. Some computer workshops are scheduled for persons who are beginner users, or who are interested in knowing more about computers, while others are designed for experienced programmers. So check with the organizers before you sign up.

Other sources of information include agricultural and trade shows where computer manufacturers often display their products, state fairs and professional conventions. At the 1983 convention of the American Society of Agronomy, for example, about 40 new microcomputer applications to agriculture were demonstrated.

Get into a class with your peers.

"Before attending a seminar or workshop, be sure it is the one that is right for you. Not all computer workshops concentrate on farming. . . . You could find yourself sitting among lawyers or bankers rather than farmers."

In the same way that you would not expect to learn how to drive a tractor by riding a motorcycle, the best self-instruction device is the computer itself. Learner programs are software that guides you step by step in learning how to use a microcomputer. As you proceed through a learner program, you answer the computer's questions and are introduced to the various features of your system. Learner programs usually begin with simple demonstrations such as helping you find keys on the keyboard. They may progress all the way to explaining how to write complex graphics software. The best learner programs let you begin using a system without having to use the manual. Some of the best learner programs include "Friendly Ware," "How to Program in the BASIC Language," and the demonstration diskette for the popular LOTUS 1-2-3 software package. Computer programs almost universally recognize the word "help," or "h," as a request for assistance. But even more important than the mere existence of a help command is the quality of the help given by the program. Help screens should be explanatory and concise, but some helps may actually be confusing. Trying out the degree and quality of the helps of a system will tell you much about its quality.

The owner's manual provided by the manufacturer is the next best source of information. Unfortunately, not all systems programmers are as successful in communicating with humans as they are with computers. Some manuals are decidedly confusing, so make sure you take a look at them before you buy. The best manufacturers publish both hardware and software guides specifically tailored to their systems. Make sure that the firm you buy from has plenty of documentation.

Microcomputer magazines (such as *Popular Computing* and *Personal Computing* for beginners and *Byte* for experienced users), newsletters (such as *Farm Computer News*) and newspaper columns can give you some useful information. They are good sources to keep updated on new equipment, learn programming tips and purchase hardware and software at reduced prices. They are no substitutes, however, for learner programs or owner's manuals.

Although some contend that books are not a good source of information, there is no question that they can serve as a reference for most microcomputer users. Computer books are the fastest-growing field in the publishing business. The average microcomputer owner will buy between 8 and 10 books. Books on hundreds of specialized microcomputer topics are now available, ranging from very simple ones to those that are targeted to the experienced user.

The table below summarizes the features of the different sources of computer instruction. The most effective learning source will depend on the users, based on their personal objectives.

A Summary of Educational Choices Available to Microcomputer Users

Type of Instruction	Examples	Comments
Formal Computer Courses	Universities Private schools Ag extensions	Provide strong background. Can be expensive in time and money.
Informal Computer Education	Friends User groups Seminars Fairs	More direct learning approach. May still require some time and money.
Do-It-Yourself Instruction	Learner programs Manuals Magazines Books	Hands-on, self-paced learning. Low cost. May be somewhat superficial.

The Future Is Dynamic and Certain

The future for personal microcomputers is bright indeed. Many of the trends and factors affecting personal computers also will be important for the farm market. Therefore, the findings of a recently completed two-year study on the future growth of personal computers, conducted at the University of Southern California, is of importance to the rural community. Some of the relevant conclusions:

- The market for consumer computers may reach 3.5 million in 1990.
- Software quality will be the decisive factor in the acceptance of consumer computers.
- Personal computers will develop rapidly in sophistication, basic capability and reliability.
- Hardware technology will continue to lead software technology in the foreseeable future.
- By the year 2000, personal computers will have extremely advanced information processing and massive information storage measured by current standards.
- The future of personal computers will depend heavily on communication and control.

During the last few years the microcomputer has moved strongly into the business world. Software systems have grown from those having limited stand-alone functionality to those with multifunctionality, integration and communication. The next few years should bring truly integrated software and hardware systems. These systems will:

- Require less technical computer expertise. More people will be using computers with less expertise. Users should not have to worry about type of operating system, management of data files or details of access methods.
- Provide more flexibility for users seeking innovation.
- Integrate such new functions as word-processing, touch input, graphic output, voice recognition, and syntheses and communications support.

The 1980's have seen an evolution from an 8-bit world (Apple II, TRS-80, Osborne I, Commodore CBM and so on) to the more powerful

16-bit microcomputers (IBM PC, Vector 4, DEC Rainbow). The role of the 8-bit has been redefined. It will be used primarily in the entry level market and will be used widely at least for the next five years. The following additional developments are expected:

- Main memory—64 bytes to 1M (million) bytes.
- Mass storage—floppy diskettes (400K) to hard disks (20M bytes), and the price of the latter will fall. This is an area where micros could never compete with mainframes and minis before.
- Operating systems.
  - Single or multiuser.
  - Multiprocessor.
- High-resolution screens.

This is the first wave of the computer tide.

"More people will be using computers with less expertise. Users should not have to worry about type of operating system, management of data files or details of access methods."

By 1985 the new generation microcomputers will appear. The new generation should overcome the slow computing speeds of the present generation, especially for updating the display. After this, at least for business applications, all hardware will be sufficiently powerful that decision-making will focus on software. Such other functions as report generation will be improved greatly by more rapid and efficient file reference.

One of the ways that personal computers will become easier for the user is that the quality of displays will be improved and more common, even on low-cost models. Resolution already is being improved, and that will continue.

Not too far in the future are several other technological features which will offer significant advantages. One of those is the touch-sensitive screen. It allows the user to select functions by touching the appropriate item on a list, or by touching some symbol representing a function rather than working from the keyboard or other input device.

Other touch-sensitive displays now under development will let users enter information simply by writing on the screen with a light pen or another special instrument.

Further down the road for widespread use is the possibility of audio input, now available on the Wang Alliance series office system. The audio workstation allows one to dictate documents using a telephone headset while at the same time seeing a graphic display on the workstation screen. The "voice document" may be stored, edited or transmitted for transcription. It is designed primarily for small local operations and could someday have application in agriculture where clerical help is rare.

To date, operating systems have been important in determining users' and software vendors' acceptance of hardware. In the field of operating systems the future will bring many new developments that will result in operating systems becoming less of a concern of the end-user. Eventually the operating systems will become transparent and more closely fused with the applications software. Those buying canned software packages will find the selection of an operating system less important, while it will remain a critical item for those writing their own application software where the speed and response time are important.

New languages will be appealing because they will incorporate familiar English commands that are easy to understand and apply. They will be self-prompting and will require only minimal training. Those languages also will provide more flexibility. The ultimate objective will be to make the user as comfortable as possible. With more memory available some systems will use a greater proportion of it for helping the user.

As with the display features, we can expect there will be improvement in the keyboards. Detachable keyboards already on the market will be adaptable to individual work habits. Low-profile keyboards with keys an inch or two above the desk will allow more comfortable placement of hands. In that area American products are going through much more rapid improvement than Japanese products.

In the future neither hardware nor software will be unique for long. Any innovative feature or concept will be incorporated rapidly in the sytem of competitors, often in a matter of months.

The most dramatic improvements will be in both quality and cost of software. There will be a wider variety, and it will be compatible with more equipment. An incompatible system is a system out of communication, and a system out of communication soon will wither away. Given that the average life of heavily used software is five years, compatibility is key. Software also will be more flexible and more forgiving in use. That is the ability to back up to where you were before you made a mistake. The new easy-to-use microcomputer software packages will enable managers

to do routine tasks more efficiently and to analyze unique problems more effectively because data, once it is in the micro, can be manipulated more easily.

Through remote and local networking, micros also will be able to access much greater data banks and handle vastly increased processing loads. Possibly with a hard disk they could offer more power and memory than a share of a mainframe.

In the future as now, buyers who choose a computer that uses cartridges and tapes as programming sources start out with a much narrower choice of programs. The cassette tapes that hold ready-made programs are physically the same for all companies. But, they still won't run on any except the computer for which they were designed. That situation may change if Japanese computer manufacturers decide on a standard cartridge and the standard then is adopted internationally.

Data processing designers are beginning to understand that the questions the users want answered are first: "Does it do the job?" and second: "Does it fit with the rest of what I have?" Criteria such as state of the art and elegant appearance have little influence on the final decision about what system to choose. Finally, now that equipment costs are down, even initial price is being subordinated to a relatively lower priority by the cost of compatibility in the mind of the wise system buyer.

What does all this mean for the farm personal computer market? There have been many glowing predictions about the future of farm computer technology. It has been reported, as an example, that agricultural accounting applications were up 569 percent in 1982, the most increase in any single industry area. Some of those predictions are suspect, but there is general agreement that the future is bright. The only real question about the growth is "how much?" A leading public expert, University of Wisconsin Professor John R. Schmidt, has stated that he doubts "anyone has an accurate feeling for the extent and speed of this development." However, like most experts, he sees the expansion as dynamic and certain.

That growth will be aided by a number of evolutionary and revolutionary developments in the field of computer technology and associated communications. The list of possibilities is almost endless in satellite, laser, fiber optic communications and cable television. As banks and other financial institutions adopt electronic banking, the home computer will save the farmer travel time and allow him or her to run the operation in a more businesslike manner.

Further, it is believed that improvements in both software and hardware will result in reduced acquisition and maintenance costs, making it cost-effective for smaller producers to purchase computers. Nevertheless, unless the farm computer owner can make effective use of the time saved through the computer, or can make the operation more cost-effective, the computer will not be a wise purchase.

They may also save mileage.

"As banks and other financial institutions adopt electronic banking, the home computer will save the farmer travel time and allow him or her to run the operation in a more businesslike manner."

Software for the farmer will continue to improve rapidly over the next few years. At first, software producers were trying to adapt existing business packages to farm programs. That can be done; however, the increased demand and volume in farm programs will result in a geometric increase in the number of customized programs designed specifically for agriculture. Five years ago nobody except government, seed and feed companies and big corporate farms were using computers. Now the kids are learning computing in school, and Mom and Dad are learning from them.

Improvement in software, in turn, will allow farmers to improve their business systems. Because most farmers used rudimentary accounting and business systems, they had to lump costs and take other actions which prevented them from properly analyzing their operations. An example is that most farmers don't go in for double-entry bookkeeping systems. In the near term, hardware purchasing patterns in rural areas probably will not change that much despite significant changes in the field as a whole. You will find some CP/M-based machines, but more often it will be Apple or Radio Shack, which are the only widespread distributors found in rural low-population areas.

Apple products, for instance, were in some 300 department stores by the end of 1983. Apple also has some 1,500 dealers in the U.S. and over 200 national account support centers. One channel of distribution Apple has eliminated is the mail-order sales approach.

DEC, Vector Graphic, Altos and Northstar are not frequently encountered in farm application. IBM is increasing its market share. After IBM introduced its personal computer in August, 1981, total sales of that machine increased to 600,000 in 1983 and are expected to reach 1 million in 1984. In 1982 Apple sold 20.3 percent of the microcomputers sold vs. 37 percent in 1981, while IBM's share of the market increased to 11 percent in 1982 from 4 percent in 1981. The IBM penetration of the rural market is progressing slowly but in the long term will be significant. The success of the IBM personal computer has resulted in the creation of a vast new array of software which is positive for agricultural users in the market.

Besides advances in hardware or software, the factor which will really make farm computers commonplace is the increased availability of support and training. Control Data, for instance, expects to open a number of regional training centers in rural areas. Many software firms are planning to hire local representatives to provide training and support at affordable cost. Those services will emphasize rapid response for the farmer who is in a crisis situation, or who cannot be distracted from production activities for administration. After all, that is why the farmer bought the computer in the beginning.

Another important development expected in the future for agriculture personal computer users is a qualitative improvement in the first line of support: written manuals. They currently vary from mediocre to bad. Too many of them are poorly indexed and not well-documented. However, now a new small growth industry is springing up to write replacement manuals for those originally issued with the equipment. That probably will not apply for the Japanese computers for which support in general is largely unknown.

Support probably will remain a problem for many in spite of the improvements noted above and the proliferation of consultants in every facet of operations. (As an example see *Leading Consultants in Computer Software* for a list of 1,200 consultants. This book is available from J. Dick & Company, 500 Hyacinth Place, Highland Park, IL 60035.) If you can find a dealer organization that understands the products, you should cherish it in the future as in the past.

There will be many changes in the future in all aspects of farm computer operations. However, the principles of equipment selection, system organization and operation will remain the same. The farmer who justifies the need for a personal computer, carefully plans, wisely buys and systematically operates will profit tremendously in the future as he or she does today.

To Buy, or Not to Buy

In the 1950's, when Sperry-Rand began marketing the first cost-effective computer systems, purchase decisions by ranchers and farmers were simple. Because those early vacuum-tube monsters were priced in the millions of dollars, they were beyond the financial capabilities of even the largest agribusiness corporation.

In addition, required software generally was unavailable in pre-packaged form. It all had to be specially programmed and written. Mechanical and electronic failures were frequent, and skilled operators were almost nonexistent. Even with the subsequent development of miniaturized electronic circuitry, costs still were high. Consequently, most farmers continued to be effectively priced out of the market.

Now all of that has changed. Rapid development of the microcomputer and required software packages has made the acquisition of a computer a real possibility for all except the smallest agribusiness people.

Still, the computer is not a prudent acquisition for ALL farmers and ranchers. Purchase decisions should be thought out carefully before actual decisions to buy are made. Mistakes in reaching those decisions can be costly, time-consuming and generally frustrating.

Where, then, to start? Probably with cost considerations, though electronic achievements during the last decade have reduced prices to a level at which they are affordable to all but the smallest farmers. More important are the needs of the purchaser. Is, for example, the operation large enough to justify the initial acquisition costs, not only of the microcomputer system itself, but also of insurance, environment and other auxiliary features?

Are neat, well-organized records important to the business? Will such records really lead to improvement? What is the value of time saved in accounting functions, letter-writing, etc.?

An intangible—but still important—consideration is the business and working habits of the prospective purchaser. Though cost-efficient from an operating standpoint, a computer acquisition would be ill-advised for an individual without the mental discipline to master the required operational techniques, or for someone unprepared to devote on a regular basis the time necessary to produce the anticipated results.

There are doubtless even more reasons for NOT purchasing a busi-

Playing computer games is nice . . . but.

"There are doubtless even more reasons for NOT purchasing a business computer for the ranch or farm. Those are numerous and range from improved cocktail party conversation to playing electronic games to keeping up with the neighbors."

ness computer for the ranch or farm. Those are numerous and range from improved cocktail party conversation to playing electronic games to keeping up with the neighbors. The best reason, however, is that a computer may be an unnecessary acquisition, considering the size and nature of the operation for which it would work. Even today, many functions can be performed more cheaply and efficiently by hand. On many small ranches and farms no more than 15 minutes or so a week routinely is devoted to bookkeeping chores.

The decision to purchase a computer, if made, is only the beginning. Now a number of related questions must be answered. Among them:

Cost—Can you afford the system necessary to do the required job? Can financing be obtained, which can be amortized out of computer-related cost reductions? And, one frequent mistake: waiting for a lower price or newer technology. If the computer is cost-effective and affordable, buy it now.

Hardware—Are memory capabilities sufficient? Can other items, such as a printer or additional disk drives, be added? Is storage capacity expandable? How much office space is available for the new system? What is the working environment of that space for both machine and operator?

Software—Will software be appropriate for the required tasks? Is it compatible with computer hardware? Can it be understood and used by existing personnel after some period of training?

Support—What about service and other assistance by the manufacturer and/or dealer? Is it available on a daily basis and, if not, can the new system be shut down safely for a longer period of time? Is the servicing organization a well-established entity, or will it be out of business six months from now? Are instruction manuals, extension service agents and computer courses readily available?

Tax considerations—Are deductions and tax credits available? What amount of net after-tax benefit would be produced by a microcomputer? How does that affect the overall economics of acquiring a computer system?

Other—Electrical power source; quality of that source; proximity of a telephone system; environmental factors, such as dust, smoke or dirt; and insurance coverage are all factors which should be considered before investing in a microcomputer system. Even if electric and telephone systems seem to be adequate, what about backup plans, especially in the more remote rural areas? Such contingency support could have a significant bearing on the total cost of a microcomputer.

Once purchased and installed in its new home, the performance of a microcomputer system is dependent largely on the dedication and enthusiasm of the owner-operator. There are thousands of time-saving functions which can be performed by today's microcomputers, but only a few of them will be useful at any given time in a particular agribusiness. The really successful operator must determine which applications are thoroughly appropriate, and then take the time needed to incorporate them into the system.

And, for continued success, the owner-operator must be prepared to continually adapt systems currently in use as well as incorporating new applications into the present format. Perhaps there may be opportunities to perform similar services on a custom basis for neighbors just the way you would contract to bale their hay or combine their corn. Several owners who purchased microcomputer systems for their own use have branched out and now are writing programs for agricultural applications similar to their own.

Someday even farm computers may listen.

"Computers will be even faster and have greater storage capacity. Operation will be simpler, perhaps even conducted at least in part by voice commands. New programs and the growing sophistication of U.S. agriculture will increase applicability."

The future will bring, almost assuredly, increased growth in many different directions. Computers will be even faster and have greater storage capacity. Operation will be simpler, perhaps even conducted at least in part by voice commands. New programs and the growing sophistication of U.S. agriculture will increase applicability. Costs, particularly when related to capability, will continue to decline.

To the prospective first-time computer user, the complexities may seem bewildering and overwhelming. Hardware choices are numerous. Literally thousands of software systems are available, and manufacturers' explanatory manuals tend to be, at best, confusing. But the big picture has not changed that much since the early days of Sperry-Rand. The purchase considerations remain essentially the same: Do I need it? Will I be able to operate it? Can I afford it? Will I really benefit by it?

The authors of this handbook welcome any comments, suggestions or additional information from readers for possible inclusion in future editions. We would especially appreciate hearing from companies whose hardware or software products may not have come to our attention during the preparation of the book. Please direct comments to:

Mr. William Windhorst
% Oppenheimer Industries
1617 Baltimore
Kansas City, MO 64108

Some Terminology to Remember

For a beginner in any activity, one of the first steps is to learn some of the terminology and rules of the game.

The new science of computing has its own language, as any farm/ranch prospective purchaser soon will discover. The following list of definitions and usages is only a starting point. It was designed to help the novice understand what is meant as he or she begins a search for a suitable microcomputer for the farm or ranch.

acoustic coupler
 A data communications device that converts electrical data signals for transmission over a telephone line using a conventional telephone headset.

acronym
 A word formed from the initial letters of the parts of a compound term.

address
 A number used in information storage or retrieval that is assigned to a specific memory location.

algorithm
 A series of instructions or procedural steps designed to result in the solution of a specific problem.

alphameric characters
 The symbol group consisting of letters (A through Z), numbers (0 through 9), punctuation marks and special characters (#, $, @).

analyst
 A person who analyzes and defines problems and develops procedures for their solution.

application software
 The instructions that direct the hardware to perform specific functions.

array
 An ordered collection of data elements, with identical attributes.

ASCII
 Acronym for "American Standard Code for Information Interchange." This is a unique seven-bit plus parity code for each letter, number, symbol and punctuation mark, established to achieve compatibility between data services.

assembler language
 A low-level programming language in which there is a one-to-one correspondence with machine code.

asynchronous transmission
Transmission of data that requires the use of start and stop elements for each character, because the interval of time between characters varies.

audit trail
A record of transactions created as a by-product of data processing runs or mechanized accounting procedure, that document the origin and flow of transactions processed through a system.

backup
The provision of facilities (duplicated files, redundant equipment, etc.) to speed the process of restart and recovery following failure.

BASIC
Acronym for "Beginner's All-purpose Symbolic Instruction Code." A high-level programming language used in most microcomputers.

batch processing
A technique in which a number of similar transactions are collected over a period of time and batched for processing as a group during a machine run.

baud
A measurement of the rate of data transmission, roughly equivalent to bits per second but with minor differences.

binary (bit)
A number system with a base of '2,' using only digits: '0' and '1.'

blocking
Combining two or more records into one block.

booting
A technique for loading a program into a computer's memory in which the program's initial instructions direct the loading of the rest of the program.

buffer
A temporary storage area for data being moved between two locations.

byte
A group of bits or binary digits processed as a unit.

character
An individual letter, numeral, or special character. In computers, characters are made up of a number of bits.

check digit
A digit added to each number in a coding system which allows for detection of errors in the recording of the code numbers.

compile
To prepare a machine language program from a high-level computer language by generating more than one machine instruction for each symbolic statement.

computer program
A series of instructions that guide the activities of a computer.

connect time
A measure of system usage by a user, from sign-on to sign-off.

conversion
> The process of changing from one method of data processing to another or from one computer system to another.

core memory
> The computer's internal information storehouse located by "addresses." Physically made up of tiny doughnut-shaped pieces of magnetizable material.

CP/M
> Control program microcomputer, an operating system developed by Digital Research. Has become an industry standard for business-oriented personal computers.

CP/M-80
> An 8-bit generation of the CP/M operating system, used on the 8080, Z80 and 8085 based microcomputers.

CP/M-86
> A 16-bit generation of the CP/M operating system, used on IBM PC.

CP/M-68
> A CP/M implementation for the Motorola 68000 series of microprocessors.

CPU
> Central Processing Unit. The heart of the computer that controls the interpretation and execution of instructions, input and output units and auxiliary attachments. Does not include interface, main memory or peripherals.

crash
> Abrupt computer failure, resulting from software or hardware malfunction.

CRT
> A television-like picture tube used in visual display terminals on which images are produced on a cathode ray tube.

cursor
> A patch of light or other visual indicator on a screen that indicates a character to be corrected or a position in which data is to be entered.

daisy wheel
> An interchangeable element impact printer producing a fully formed character.

data
> The input of facts, numbers, letters and symbols that a computer processes.

data base (data base management system)
> A systematic approach to storage, updating and retrieval of information stored as data items, usually in the form of records in a file, where many users will use common data banks.

data file (file)
> A collection of related data records organized in a specific manner.

data link
> Any form of technology that permits a signal to travel between two locations: communications lines, modems or even a satellite link.

debug
> To find mistakes or problems with a program and then eliminate them.

desktop computer
A personal computer designed to fit within the working surface of a desk.

digit
A character used to designate a quantity.

direct-access
A basic type of storage medium which allows information to be accessed by positioning the medium or accessing mechanism directly to the information required, thus permitting direct addressing of data locations.

disk drive
A piece of equipment used to store and access data that is connected to the CPU and feeds signals from the disk to the computer and back.

diskette
A flexible or floppy disk. A magnetic coated mylar disk enclosed in a protective envelope used to store information.

display
The information on a video screen.

documentation
Written instructions that tell you how to use computer hardware or software.

DOS
Disk Operating System. A program that utilizes disks and coordinates the operations of a computer system.

dot-matrix
A printer type using a number of pins impacting a ribbon to form characters.

duplex
Simultaneous two-way independent transmission in both directions.

8-bit
Refers to the number of bits in a word that can be processed, stored and recalled at one time in one machine cycle.

8080
An 8-bit system developed by Intel.

8088
A 16-bit internal structure and an 8-bit external structure.

8085
A faster version of the Intel 8080.

8086
A 16-bit microprocessor produced by Intel.

electronic spreadsheet
A program that acts like a multicolumn accounting worksheet to add columns of data down and across, automatically calculating totals, percentages and carry forward amounts.

field
A data item that serves a similar function in all records of that group.

file

> An organized, named collection of records treated as a unit, usually arranged in some sequence.

firmware

> A program stored in the computer's permanent memory, or ROM. Since such a program doesn't have to be re-entered every time the computer is turned on, it is "harder" than software.

floppy disk

> See *diskette*.

flowchart

> A diagram representing the logical flow of a program or system.

font

> A character set in a particular style and size of type.

game port

> A small computer port used to attach joysticks, game paddles or light pens.

generation four

> Artificial intelligence. Computers that simulate human intelligence by learning, reasoning, adapting or self-correcting.

generation one

> From 1951, the first commercially produced machines. Use of vacuum tubes.

generation three

> From 1964, integrated circuitry. Introduction of minicomputers and very fast core.

generation two

> From 1958, transistor technology. Introduction of data communications over telephone lines.

GIGO

> Garbage In, Garbage Out. Output from a computer is only as good as the data input.

grandfather backup

> A process in which backup is rotated among three sets of diskettes.

graphics

> Facilities to provide computer output in the form of displays, drawings and pictures.

half duplex

> Two-way data transmission in which data transfers occur alternately in both directions, but not simultaneously.

hard copy

> Information generated by a computer and printed on paper.

hard disk

> A rigid, random access, high-capacity magnetic storage medium.

hardware

> The physical components of a computer system.

hardwired
Pertaining to a processing system employing wired circuitry to implement system functions.

hash total
An arithmetic total of data used for checking the accuracy of one or more corresponding fields of a file.

hexadecimal
A number system with a base of "16"; valid digits range from 0 through F.

home computer
A computer whose main function is game playing, with a minor amount of personal computing on the side. This is an inexpensive system that can be connected to your TV.

ink jet printer
A non-impact printing technique which utilizes droplets of ink, placing them precisely to form individual print characters.

input
The data to be processed.

input device
A device such as a card reader, CRT, teletypewriter, etc., which converts data into electronic signals that can be interpreted by the computer.

inquiry
A request for information from storage.

instruction
The coded command that specifies the type of operation which should take place.

interactive
Pertaining to an application in which each entry elicits a response.

interface
A place inside or outside a computer where various components meet.

interpreter
A program that translates and executes each source language statement before translating and executing the next one.

I/O
Input/output. The general term used in describing the flow of information to and from the computer.

I/O bound
Pertaining to programs with a large number of I/O operations which result in much wasted CPU time. Input/output operations are much slower than CPU processing time.

joystick
A game control stick or lever used to change the position of the cursor or other position marker on a display screen.

K (kilobyte)
Conventionally, 1,000 bytes. Actually, 1K is 1,024 bytes.

language
A means of translating commands phrased in English into something a computer can understand.

letter-quality printer
A printer which forms whole characters and provides output much like a standard office typewriter in quality.

loop
In programming, a group of instructions that return to the starting point and repeat themselves until a predetermined count or other test is satisfied.

low-level language
A programming language in which instructions have a one-to-one relationship with machine code.

machine cycle
The basic operating cycle of a CPU during which a single instruction is fetched, decoded and executed.

machine-independent
Pertaining to procedures or programs created without regard for the actual devices that will be used to process them.

machine language
A binary language all digital computers must use.

main storage
The general-purpose program addressable storage of a computer where program instructions and data are retained for active use in the system.

mainframe
1. The physical structure that holds the CPU of a microcomputer. 2. The largest of computers with an expansive internal memory and fast processing time. These computers are much more expensive than microcomputers or minicomputers.

master file
A main reference file of information used in a computer system.

matrix printer
A printer which forms characters by printing a pattern of dots.

megabyte
Conventionally 1 million bytes; usually $1,024 \times 1,024$ bytes.

memory
That portion of the computer which is used to store information.

menu
A displayed list of options from which the user selects an action to be performed by typing a number or by positioning the cursor.

microcomputer
A small computer utilizing a microprocessor.

microprocessor
The central unit of microcomputer that contains the logical elements for manipulating data and performing arithmetical or logical operations on it.

minicomputer
A type of computer whose physical size is smaller and more modular than mainframes. In general, its performance exceeds that of a microcomputer.

modem
Acronym for "modulator-demodulator." A device that permits one computer to communicate with another via telephone, using computer-generated tones.

modulation
In data communications, the process by which some characteristic of a high-frequency carrier signal is varied in accordance with another, lower-frequency "information" signal. Used in data sets to make computer terminal signals compatible with communication facilities.

MS-DOS
An operating system developed by Microsoft and Seattle Computer for 16-bit systems.

multiplexer (multiplexing)
A hardware device that allows handling of multiple low-speed signals over a single high-speed channel.

multiprogramming
A computer operating system that can handle two or more computer programs at the same time.

nanosecond
One billionth of a second.

network
A computer communications system consisting of one or more terminals communicating with a single host computer system.

noise
Undesirable signals bearing no desired information, and frequently capable of introducing errors into the communication process.

OEM
Original equipment manufacturer. A company or organization that purchases computers and peripheral equipment for use as components that can be integrated into a complete system by adding software or additional hardware.

on-line
1. Pertaining to the operation of peripherals or terminals in direct interactive communication and under control of the CPU via a communication channel. 2. Pertaining to a user's ability to interact with a computer via either the console or a terminal.

operating system
A set of very complex computer programs normally supplied by the vendor that controls, monitors and executes programs.

output
Any data that comes out of a computer system or any of its parts.

output device
A device such as a printer or monitor which takes information from the computer and turns it into usable form.

parallel
The simultaneous transfer of a group of binary bits. The distance is limited but faster than serial transmission.

party bit
Used to check that data has been transmitted accurately. Adding a bit to a unit of information so as to maintain the total number of 1's in that unit, always odd or always even, depending upon which method is chosen.

PC-DOS
IBM's version of MS-DOS for the IBM Personal Computer.

peripheral equipment
Any external (to the CPU) piece of equipment that receives information from or sends it to a computer. Examples are disk drives, magnetic tape, CRT's, printers and modems.

personal computer
A computer that is generally low in cost, based on a particular micro-processor and too small to be shared while in use.

polling
A scheme in which a central unit chooses one remote unit after another and exchanges data with each remote unit that has information ready.

portable computer
A microcomputer system's electronic components integrated and packed in a case small and light enough to be easily transported.

preventive maintenance
Precautionary measures taken on a system to forestall failures, by providing for systematic inspection, detection and correction of early problems before they develop into major defects.

primary storage
See *main storage*.

printer
A peripheral that prints out hard copy.

program
A series of instructions that tells a computer in detail how to process data.

RAM
Random access memory. A type of memory that provides immediate access to any storage location. Information is usually transferred into RAM from permanent storage and is lost when the power is turned off.

random access
The ability to gain access to any one storage location among many using an equal amount of time and effort and not depending upon any previous action.

real-time
The processing of transactions as they occur rather than batching them.

register
> A memory device capable of containing one or more computer bits or words. The register is usually found in the CPU.

ROM
> Read only memory. This is permanent memory that is built into the computer and cannot be altered during normal computer use.

RS-232-C
> A technical specification published by the Electronic Industries Association establishing the interface requirements between modems and terminals or computers.

sequential
> In numeric sequence, normally in ascending order.

serial
> The transfer of bits in sequential order, one right after the other.

service bureau
> A company that supplies users with batch or interactive processing either on-line or off-line. Typical applications would include payroll, billing and bookkeeping.

16-bit
> Refers to the number of bits in a word that can be processed, stored and recalled at one time in one machine cycle.

68000
> A 32-bit internal and 16-bit external word length microprocessor developed by Motorola.

6502
> An 8-bit word length microprocessor developed by MOS Technology.

softcard
> A circuit board made by Microsoft, Inc., which enables an Apple to use the CP/M-80 operating system.

software
> Stored sets of instructions contained in a program which govern the operation of a computer system and make the hardware run.

sort
> A processing run or operation to distribute data in numeric, alphabetic or alphameric groups according to a given standard or rule.

source program
> The original language version of a program as it was prepared by a programmer. It will be converted to an object code before execution by the computer.

storage
> A computer-oriented medium in which data is retained. Primary or main storage is the internal storage area where data and program instructions are retained for active use in the system. External storage is for less active data and may include magnetic tape, disk or diskette.

synchronization

Data transfer that contains timing information along with the bit-by-bit information flow.

systems analysis (analyst)

Complete analysis of all activity phases of an organization to determine precisely what must be accomplished and how to accomplish it.

telecommunications

Data transmission between a computing system and remotely located
devices via a unit that performs the necessary format conversion and controls the rate of transmission.

templates

A preprogrammed set of formulas and report formats which are used in
conjunction with an electronic spreadsheet program and apply to a specific
decision situation.

32-bit

Refers to the number of bits in a word that can be processed, stored and
recalled at one time in one machine cycle.

time sharing

A method of operation in which the resources of a computer facility are
shared by several users at the same time via terminals, making it appear that
the users are all handled simultaneously.

TRS-80

A popular microcomputer manufactured by Radio Shack which uses a Z80
microprocessor.

turnkey system

A system in which the vendor provides for system design and installation,
and supplies all necessary hardware, software and documentation elements.

Unix

A multiuser operating system developed by Bell Laboratories.

user group

An organization made up of users that gives them an opportunity to share
knowledge, to exchange programs and to jointly influence vendor software
and hardware support and policy.

utility program

A specialized program performing a frequently required everyday task, for
example, sorting, file dump.

VDT

Video display terminal—see *CRT.*

vendor

A company that supplies material.

videotex

Used to describe many different kinds of services that can deliver text and
sometimes crude graphics to the video screen or a television, data terminal
or microcomputer.

VisiCalc
> An electronic spreadsheet. Simulates a spreadsheet format on the computer screen.

winchester disk
> A form of hard disk permanently sealed into a case along with the read/write heads and head actuator.

word
> A group of binary digits that occupy one storage location in a computer.

Z80
> An 8-bit microprocessor developed by Zilog, Inc.

APPENDIX A

Directory of Available Support

AGRICULTURAL COMPUTER BOOKS

All About On-Farm Computing (AgriData Resources, Inc.)

Agriware Company
3426 Wyndcrest Drive
Elko, MN 55020

$19.75

Computers in Farming (Steven T. Sonka)

McGraw-Hill Book Co.
Manchester Road
Manchester, MO 63011

$19.95

Farm Computer Guide

Successful Farming
1716 Locust St.
Des Moines, IA 50336

$3.95

Microcomputers on the Farm (Jack O. Beasley)

Howard W. Sams & Co., Inc.
4300 W. 62nd St.
Indianapolis, IN 46206

$14.95

AGRICULTURAL COMPUTER PERIODICALS

AgriComp

AgriComp
103 Outdoor Building
Columbia, MO 62501

$15.00/yr. (6 issues)

Agricultural Computing

Doane-Western, Inc.
11701 Borman Drive
St. Louis, MO 63146

$48.00/yr. (12 issues)

Computer Farming Newsletter
> P.O. Box 22642
> Memphis, TN 38122-0642
> $33.00/yr. (12 issues)

Farm Computer News
> Successful Farming
> Farm Computer News
> 1716 Locust St.
> Des Moines, IA 50336
> $40.00/yr. (12 issues)

AGRICULTURAL SOFTWARE LISTINGS

AGPROS Micro Systems
> P.O. Box 64539
> Lubbock, TX 79464
> From $95.00 to $295.00

Agricultural Software Directory (for Apple)
> Agriware Company
> 3426 Wyndcrest Drive
> Elko, MN 55020
> $19.95

Farm Software Guide
> Successful Farming
> 1716 Locust St.
> Des Moines, IA 50336
> $4.50

TRS-80 Agricultural Software Sourcebook
> Radio Shack
> $2.95

Updated Inventory of Agricultural Computer Programs
> Food and Resource Economics Dept.
> Cooperative Extension Service
> Administrative Services
> University of Florida
> Gainesville, FL 32611
> $3.50

GENERAL PURPOSE AND AGRICULTURAL
SOFTWARE LISTINGS

LIST
Redgate Publishing Co.
$12.50

Vanlove's 1984 Apple II/III Software Directory
Advanced Software Technology, Inc.
$24.95

NETWORKS (DIAL-UP SERVICES)

AACS
American Agricultural Communications Systems, Inc.
225 Touhy Ave.
Park Ridge, IL 60068
312/399-5700

AGNET
105 Miller Hall
University of Nebraska
Lincoln, NE 68583-0713
402/472-1892

AgriStar
205 West Highland Ave.
Milwaukee, WI 53203
414/278-7676

AT&T Information Systems
Attn.: Jim Vance, 3rd floor
7201 Metro Blvd.
Edina, MN 55435
612/828-5367

CMN
Computerized Management Network
Plaza 1, Building D
Virginia Tech. Extension Division
Blacksburg, VA 24061
703/961-6705

CompuServe
Consumer Information Services
2180 Wilson Road
Columbus, OH 43228
614/457-8650

Harris Electronic News
300 W. 2nd
Hutchinson, KS 67501
316/662-8667

Instant Update
Professional Farmers of America
219 Parkade
Cedar Falls, IA 50613
319/277-1278

The Source
1616 Anderson Road
McLean, VA 22102
703/734-7500

SERVICE BUREAUS

Control Data's Agricultural Community Services
P.O. Box 35423
Minneapolis, MN 55435
612/853-6974

Farm Bureau Agricultural Business Corp.
5400 University Ave.
West Des Moines, IA 50265
515/225-5658

Production Credit Association
(see your local association)

Professional Swine Records
P.O. Box 158
Graceville, MN 56240
612/748-7501

TURNKEY SYSTEMS

Computone
One Dunwoody Park
Atlanta, GA 30338
404/393-3010

Farmland Industries, Inc.
Dept. 169
P.O. Box 7305
Kansas City, MO 64116
816/459-6033

On-Farm Computing, Inc.
5950 W. Raymond St.
Indianapolis, IN 46241

317/247-5179

OT Industries, Inc.
332 Chester St.
St. Paul, MN 55107

612/227-3174

Valmont Industries, Inc.
Agricultural Management Systems Division
Valley, NE 68064

402/359-2201

APPENDIX B

Agricultural Software Listing

General Management

General Accounting

Crops

Livestock

Equipment/Supplies

Poultry

Other

Dairy

Educational

Abbreviations:

TI	Texas Instruments
TRS	(Tandy) Radio Shack
CPM	CP/M
IBM	IBM Personal Computer or MS-DOS
Datamaster	IBM S/23 Datamaster

For specific computer models and additional information, contact vendors. Names, addresses and telephone numbers can be found in Appendix C.

Title (Description) and Vendor	Operating System or Computer	Approx. Price
— General Management —		
Ag Managers Tool Kit Offered by: Farmplan	Apple	$ 225
Ag-Planner Offered by: Countryside Data	CPM, Digital	$ 450
Agri-Plus (financial management program) Offered by: Comtech	CPM, IBM	$ 995
AgriCalc (11 worksheets) Offered by: McIntosh Software *need VisiCalc*	Apple	$ 125
Agricultural Decision Aids Offered by: OT Industries, Inc.	Farmi	$ 250
Agricultural Software Package (35 decision aids) Offered by: Wisconsin Microware (Ag Pac)	Apple, IBM, Digital	$1500
Business Management Offered by: Harris Technical Systems	Apple, IBM, Digital	$ 95
Business Management Aids Offered by: Farm Information Services, Inc.	Apple	$ 95
Capital Investment Analysis Offered by: Brubaker & Associates, Inc.	IBM, Digital	$ 195
Capital Sales Analysis Offered by: Brubaker & Associates, Inc.	IBM	$ 295
The Combination Big Grain & Hog Farmer Offered by: Farm Information Services, Inc.	Apple	$1560

Title (Description) and Vendor	Operating System or Computer	Approx. Price
The Combination Grain & Hog Farmer Offered by: Farm Information Services, Inc.	Apple	$1290
Crew Option (crew processing & reporting) Offered by: Compufarm	CPM	$ 600
Crop/Livestock Profit Projector Offered by: Harris Technical Systems	Apple, IBM, Digital	$ 110
Crops, Machinery, Irrigation Package #1 Offered by: Texas Agricultural Extension Service *Texans price*	CPM	$ 60
F.A.R.M. Aids (VisiCalc templates) Offered by: Hobar Publications *need VisiCalc*	Apple, IBM	$ 60
Farm Analysis System Summary Offered by: Ag-Data, Inc.	CPM	$ 495
Farm Analyst Offered by: Harvest Computer Systems *need 132-col. printer*	Apple	$ 80
Farm Analyst II Offered by: Harvest Computer Systems *need 132-col. printer*	Apple	$ 180
Farm & Grower Payroll Offered by: Micro-Crop	Apple, TRS, CPM, IBM	$ 400
Farm Business Analysis Offered by: Hobar Publications	Apple	$ 30
Farm Decision Aids Offered by: Decision Data & Services, Inc.	Apple	$ 195
Farm Decision Aids Package Offered by: Hobar Publications	Apple	$ 150
Farm Inventory Offered by: Red Wing Business Systems	Apple, TRS, IBM	$ 250

Title (Description) and Vendor	Operating System or Computer	Approx. Price
Farm Management Offered by: Pearlsoft	CPM	$ 750
Farm Manager (beef production) Offered by: Cyberia, Inc.	Commodore	$ 50
Farm Manager (general business) Offered by: Cyberia, Inc.	Commodore	$ 50
Farm Manager (pork production) Offered by: Cyberia, Inc.	Commodore	$ 50
Farm Package Offered by: Ag-tronics Associates	Apple	$ 75
Farm Profit Plan Crop Model Offered by: Brubaker & Associates, Inc.	IBM, Digital	$ 995
Farm Profitability Analysis Offered by: Hobar Publications	Apple	$ 40
Farm Profitability Decisions Offered by: Successful Farming	Apple, TRS	$ 89
Farm Record Management Offered by: Picton Farm Computers *16K or larger*	TRS	$ 25
Farm Record Sort Offered by: Picton Farm Computers *16K or larger*	TRS	$ 25
Farm Simulator (simulates farm finances) Offered by: Duane Bristow—Albany, Ky.	TRS	$ 35
Farmer's Workbook Offered by: Cyberia, Inc.	Commodore	$ 250
Farms System (financial management) Offered by: Systems for Management Information	IBM, TI	$1275
Farmware (provides mgt. info.) Offered by: Fred's Micro-ware	Apple, TRS	$ 149
Financial Decisions Offered by: Successful Farming	Apple, TRS	$ 89

AGRICULTURAL COMPUTER GUIDE & DIRECTORY

Title (Description) and Vendor	Operating System or Computer	Approx. Price
The Financial Manager TM Program Offered by: Farm Management System	TRS, CPM, Victor, Vector Graphic, IBM, Digital	$1450
Labor Distribution & Employee History Offered by: Micro-Crop	Apple, TRS, CPM, IBM	$ 500
Land Lease Offered by: Harvest Computer Systems	Apple	$ 80
Livestock-Crop-Finance Management Programs Offered by: Ag Plus Software	Apple	$ 90
Management Cost Accounting Offered by: Agdata	TRS, CPM, Vector Graphic, IBM	$ 495
Management Decision: Grow Corn or Soybeans . . . Offered by: Hobar Publications	Apple	$ 30
Moveaverage (charting program) Offered by: Oklahoma State U. Dept. of Ag. Econ.	TRS	$ 20
New '83 Releases Package #1 Net Present Value Irr. Offered by: Texas Agricultural Extension Service *Texans price*	CPM	$ 30
Piecework (payroll) Offered by: Micro-Crop	Apple, TRS, CPM, IBM	$ 600
Record Management System (financial) Offered by: Frontier	CPM, IBM	$2995
Record Management Offered by: Oklahoma State U. Dept. of Ag. Econ.	TRS	$ 15
Worksheet Offered by: Harvest Computer Systems *VisiCalc-Multiplan*	Apple, IBM	$ 75

Title (Description) and Vendor	Operating System or Computer	Approx. Price
– General Accounting –		
Accounting Offered by: Agri-Management Services, Inc.	CPM, IBM	$ 595
Accounting Offered by: Micro Spike	CPM	$ 750
Accounting Package Offered by: Harris Technical Systems	Apple, IBM, Digital	$ 650
Accounts Payable Offered by: Dairy Herd Management Services, Inc.	Apple, TRS, CPM, Victor, IBM, Altos	$1095
Accounts Payable Offered by: Red Wing Business Systems	Apple, TRS, IBM, Digital	$ 250
Accounts Payable Offered by: Micro-Crop	Apple, TRS, CPM, IBM	$1000
Accounts Receivable Offered by: Dairy Herd Management Services, Inc.	Apple, TRS, CPM, Victor, IBM, Altos	$1095
Accounts Receivable Offered by: Red Wing Business Systems	Apple, TRS, IBM, Digital	$ 400
Accounts Receivable Offered by: Pearlsoft	CPM	$ 495
Accounts Receivable Offered by: Micro-Crop	Apple, TRS, CPM, IBM	$ 300
Accounts Receivable—Large Offered by: Farm Information Services, Inc.	Apple	$ 950
Accounts Receivable—Small Offered by: Farm Information Services, Inc.	Apple	$ 750
Activity Costs (acct.) Offered by: Compufarm	CPM	$1200
Ag/Billing/Inventory Offered by: Micro-Crop	Apple, TRS, CPM, IBM	$2000

Title (Description) and Vendor	Operating System or Computer	Approx. Price
Ag-Finance Offered by: Countryside Data	CPM, Digital	$ 750
Ag-Pilot (record-keeping) Offered by: Farm Information Services, Inc.	Apple	$ 675
Agri-Enterprise Accounting Offered by: Hi-Plains Systems, Inc.	CPM, IBM, Victor	$ 495
Agri-Ledger (ag. acct. system) Offered by: Small Business Computer Systems	Apple, IBM	$ 550
All Star Accounting System Offered by: Terrell Brothers (All Star computer)	TRS	$ 895
Asset Management Offered by: Red Wing Business Systems	Apple, TRS, IBM, Digital	$ 250
The Assistant CPA of Agriculture Offered by: Farm Information Services, Inc.	Apple	$ 475
The Aurora (inventory, invoicing, accts. rcvble., etc.) Offered by: Compufarm	CPM	$6000
Bookkeeping System Offered by: Successful Farming	Apple, TRS, IBM	$ 500
Budgeting—Cash Flow Projections Offered by: Computerized Farm Info. Systems, Inc.	Apple, IBM	$ 400
Bulk Fuel & Oil Distributor (accts. rcvble. set-up) Offered by: Farm Information Services, Inc.	Apple	$ 950
The Business Controller Offered by: Farm Information Services, Inc.	Apple	$1500
Cash Flo Offered by: Iowa Farm Business Association	Apple	$ 80
Cash Flow Offered by: Homestead Computer Company	Vector Graphic, IBM	$ 195

Title (Description) and Vendor	Operating System or Computer	Approx. Price
Cash Flow Plan Offered by: Duane Bristow—Albany, Ky.	TRS	$ 45
Check Register System Offered by: Ag-Data, Inc.	CPM	$ 295
Comfab (computerized farm bookkeeping) Offered by: F.A.R.M. Computer Consulting	Apple, TRS, IBM	$ 600
Computerized Farm Accounting System Offered by: Ag-Com	Apple	$ 450
Computerized Farm Records Offered by: Micro Learningware	Apple, TRS	$ 149
Cost Acct., Vendor Payment, A/R, Cost Estimation Offered by: Haskell & Associates	CPM	$1050
The CPA of Agriculture (complete personal acctnt.) Offered by: Farm Information Services, Inc.	Apple	$ 750
Cyber-Farmer (farm accounting) Offered by: Cyberia, Inc.	Commodore	$ 450
Cyber-Farmer (farm acct. on Commodore 64) Offered by: Cyberia, Inc.	Commodore	$ 195
Depreciation Log Offered by: Harvest Computer Systems *need 132-col. printer*	Apple	$ 175
Depreciation Plus Offered by: FBS Systems	Apple, TRS, CPM, IBM	$ 295
Dynamic Farm Accountant Offered by: Ag-tronics Associates	Apple	$ 300
Enterprising (optional Confab program) Mult. Farms Offered by: F.A.R.M. Computer Consulting	Apple, TRS, IBM	$ 150

Title (Description) and Vendor	Operating System or Computer	Approx. Price
Estate Tax Offered by: Oklahoma State U. Dept. of Ag. Econ.	TRS	$ 20
FACS (Farm Accounting Control System) Offered by: Vertical Software, Inc.	Apple, IBM	$ 525
F.A.R.M. Commercial (for use by accountants) Offered by: Specialized Data Systems, Inc.	Apple	$ 995
F.A.R.M. on Farm (one-farm family) Offered by: Specialized Data Systems, Inc.	Apple	$ 395
Farm Account Offered by: Fred's Micro-ware	Apple, TRS	$ 100
Farm Accountant Offered by: Ag-tronics Associates	Apple	$ 200
Farm Accounting & Records Mgt. Offered by: Hobar Publications	Apple	$ 165
Farm Accounting Package Offered by: Hobar Publications	Apple	$ 265
Farm Accounting System Offered by: Farmhand Computer Systems, Inc.	CPM	$ 995
Farm Database Financial Analysis & Records Offered by: Duane Bristow—Albany, Ky. *4 programs*	TRS	$ 195
Farm Enterprise Analysis Offered by: Duane Bristow—Albany, Ky.	TRS	$ 70
Farm Inventory Offered by: Systems for Management Information	IBM, TI	$ 295
Farm Ledger Offered by: Farm Computer Systems *need 80-col. printer*	TRS, IBM	$ 295

Title (Description) and Vendor	Operating System or Computer	Approx. Price
Farm Ledger Offered by: Harvest Computer Systems	Apple, IBM, Victor	$ 250
Farm Management Accounting System Offered by: IBM	Datamaster	$3000
Farm Management Accounting System Offered by: Farm Management Systems of Mississippi, Inc.	IBM	$ 475
Farm Management Billing Offered by: Agdata	TRS, CPM, Vector Graphic, IBM	$ 495
Farm Operating Loan Calculation Offered by: Picton Farm Computers *16K or larger*	TRS	$ 25
Farm Record Cash Flow Offered by: Picton Farm Computers *16K or larger*	TRS	$ 25
Farmplan Bookkeeper Offered by: Farmplan	Apple	$ 395
Farmrecord Offered by: Oklahoma State U. Dept. of Ag. Econ.	TRS	$ 40
Finance Package #1 Offered by: Texas Agricultural Extension Service *Texans price*	CPM	$ 30
Financial Management Series I Offered by: Harris Technical Systems	Apple, IBM, Digital	$ 155
Financial Package Offered by: Farmplan	Apple, TI	$1200
Fixed Asset Accounting Offered by: Haskell & Associates	CPM	$ 600
Fixed Assets Offered by: Homestead Computer Company	Vector Graphic, IBM	$ 295
General Ledger Offered by: Dairy Herd Management Services, Inc.	Apple, TRS, CPM, Victor, IBM, Altos	$1095

Title (Description) and Vendor	Operating System or Computer	Approx. Price
General Ledger Offered by: Computerized Farm Info. Systems, Inc.	Apple, IBM	$ 600
General Ledger Offered by: Agdata	TRS, CPM, Vector Graphic, IBM	$ 995
General Ledger Offered by: Pearlsoft	CPM	$ 495
General Ledger Offered by: Red Wing Business Systems	Apple, TRS, IBM, Digital	$ 500
General Ledger Offered by: Micro-Crop	Apple, TRS, CPM, IBM	$1000
General Ledger Offered by: Homestead Computer Company	Vector Graphic, IBM	$ 695
General Ledger by Profit Center Offered by: Duane Bristow—Albany, Ky.	TRS	$ 195
Grower Payables Offered by: Micro-Crop	Apple, TRS, CPM, IBM	$ 500
Huller Billing Offered by: Agdata	TRS, CPM, Vector Graphic, IBM	$ 495
Inventory Offered by: Pearlsoft	CPM	$ 295
Inventory Offered by: Homestead Computer Company	Vector Graphic, IBM	$ 295
IRA Projections Offered by: Decision Data & Services, Inc.	Apple	$ 125
Key Systems Accountability Software Offered by: Dairy Herd Management Services, Inc.	Apple, TRS, CPM, Victor, IBM, Altos	$3995
Level 1 Accounting System Offered by: Reaper Software Company, Inc.	Apple	$ 495
Loan Offered by: Oklahoma State U. Dept. of Ag. Econ.	Apple, TRS	$ 10

Title (Description) and Vendor	Operating System or Computer	Approx. Price
Loan Profitability Offered by: Decision Data & Services, Inc.	Apple	$ 225
Loan Repayment—Amortization Program Offered by: Ag Plus Software	Apple	$ 35
Micro Manager Farm Accounting & Inventory Control Offered by: OT Industries, Inc.	Farmi	$1450
Micro Mars (accounting package) Offered by: Iowa Farm Business Association	Apple	$ 350
Micro-computer Tools for Auditors Offered by: Haskell & Associates	CPM	$ 188
Order Entry & Receivables Offered by: Agri-Management Services, Inc.	CPM, IBM	$1195
Packing Shed Offered by: Agdata	TRS, CPM, Vector Graphic, IBM	$ 995
Payroll Offered by: Farm Information Services, Inc.	Apple	$ 225
Payroll Offered by: Dairy Herd Management Services, Inc.	Apple, TRS, CPM, Victor, IBM, Altos	$1095
Payroll Offered by: Compufarm	CPM	$2000
Payroll Offered by: Agri-Management Services, Inc.	CPM, IBM	$ 595
Payroll Offered by: Agdata	TRS, CPM, Vector Graphic, IBM	$ 995
Payroll Offered by: Pearlsoft	CPM	$ 395
Payroll Offered by: Red Wing Business Systems	Apple, TRS, IBM, Digital	$ 250

Title (Description) and Vendor	Operating System or Computer	Approx. Price
Payroll (optional Confab program) Offered by: F.A.R.M. Computer Consulting	Apple, TRS, IBM	$ 150
Piece Rate Payroll Offered by: Farm Management Systems of Mississippi, Inc.	Datamaster	$2000
Producer Accountant Offered by: Decision Data & Services, Inc.	Apple	$ 500
Professional Time Mgt., A/R, Billing System Offered by: Haskell & Associates	CPM	$ 950
Purveyor (wholesale produce) Offered by: Micro-Crop	Apple, TRS, CPM, IBM	$4000
Resource Records Offered by: Homestead Computer Company	Vector Graphic, IBM	$ 195
Sales Analysis Offered by: Micro-Crop	Apple, TRS, CPM, IBM	$ 300
Screen Budget Offered by: Oklahoma State U. Dept. of Ag. Econ.	TRS	$ 20
Simpler Payroll Offered by: Compufarm	CPM	$ 600
Transaction (bookkeeping) Offered by: FBS Systems	Apple, TRS, CPM, IBM, Digital, TI	$ 695
VisiCalc Ag. Templates Offered by: Ag-tronics Associates	Apple	$ 50
W-2 Form Program Offered by: Farm Information Services, Inc.	Apple	$ 25

— *Crops* —

Accounting (specialized to crops) Offered by: Agri-Management Services, Inc.	CPM, IBM	$ 595
The Big Cotton Farmer Special Offered by: Farm Information Services, Inc.	Apple	$1195

Title (Description) and Vendor	Operating System or Computer	Approx. Price
The Big Grain Farmer Special Offered by: Farm Information Services, Inc.	Apple	$1250
Breakeven Analysis for Crops Offered by: Farm Information Services, Inc.	Apple	$ 75

The Combination Big Cotton and
  Grain Farmer
Offered by: Farm Information
  Services, Inc.
	Apple	$1395

The Combination Cotton and Grain
  Farmer
Offered by: Farm Information
  Services, Inc.
	Apple	$1125

Corn CPA Offered by: Fred's Micro-ware	Apple, TRS	$ 20
Corn Crop Disk (irrigation) Offered by: Climate Assessment Technology, Inc.	Apple, TRS, IBM	$ 245
Corn Crop Disk (non-irrigation) Offered by: Climate Assessment Technology, Inc.	Apple, TRS, IBM	$ 125
Corn/Soybean Series I Offered by: Harris Technical Systems	Apple, IBM	$ 155
Corn Storage Data Management Offered by: Computerized Farm Info. Systems, Inc.	Apple	$1000
Cost per Acre Offered by: Micro Learningware	TRS	$ 25
The Cotton Farmer Special Offered by: Farm Information Services, Inc.	Apple	$ 945
Cotton Gin Offered by: Farm Information Services, Inc.	Apple	$1250
Cotton Loan Offered by: Farm Information Services, Inc.	Apple	$ 175

Title (Description) and Vendor	Operating System or Computer	Approx. Price
Cotton PIK (figures loan values, weight for PIK lbs., etc.) Offered by: Farm Information Services, Inc.	Apple	$ 95
Cotton Sort Offered by: Farm Information Services, Inc.	Apple	$ 175
Crop Accounting Offered by: Compufarm	CPM	$1200
Crop Budget Analysis Offered by: Hobar Publications	Apple	$ 40
Crop Control Offered by: Decision Data & Services, Inc.	Apple	$ 550
Crop Costing System Offered by: IBM	Datamaster	$2000
Crop Costing System Offered by: Farm Management Systems of Mississippi, Inc.	IBM	$1000
Crop Decisions Offered by: Successful Farming	Apple, TRS	$ 89
Crop Management Offered by: Micro-Crop	Apple, TRS, CPM, IBM	$1250
Crop Management Offered by: Harris Technical Systems	Apple, IBM, Digital	$ 95
Crop Package Offered by: Farmplan	Apple, TI	$ 950
Crop Planning Offered by: Homestead Computer Company	Vector Graphic, IBM	$ 125
Crop Production Analysis Offered by: Ag Plus Software	Apple	$ 110
Crop Production Analysis Offered by: Ag-Com	Apple	$ 50
Crop Record Keeping Offered by: Harris Technical Systems	Apple, IBM, Digital	$ 650

Title (Description) and Vendor	Operating System or Computer	Approx. Price
Crop Recordkeeping Offered by: Homestead Computer Company	Vector Graphic, IBM	$ 375
Crop Records System Offered by: Ag-tronics Associates	Apple	$ 100
Cropmaster Offered by: Professional Farm Software	TRS, CPM	$ 750
Crops (management) Offered by: Agri-Management Services, Inc.	CPM, IBM	$ 995
Farm Weather Center (master disk) Offered by: Climate Assessment Technology, Inc.	Apple, TRS, IBM	$ 295
Field & Crop Offered by: Computerized Farm Info. Systems, Inc.	Apple, IBM	$1250
Field Costs Offered by: Compufarm	CPM	$1600
Field Inventory Offered by: Fred's Micro-ware	Apple, TRS	$ 25
Field Manager Offered by: Harvest Computer Systems	Apple	$ 350
Field Program (cropping info.) Offered by: Micro Spike	CPM	$ 500
Government Program Offered by: Oklahoma State U. Dept. of Ag. Econ.	TRS	$ 20
Grain Contracts & Inventory Offered by: Farm Information Services, Inc.	Apple	$ 225
The Grain Farmer Special Offered by: Farm Information Services, Inc.	Apple	$ 975
Grain Storage Offered by: Oklahoma State U. Dept. of Ag. Econ.	Apple, TRS	$ 10

Title (Description) and Vendor	Operating System or Computer	Approx. Price
Herbicide Selection Offered by: Successful Farming	Apple, TRS	$ 125
Insecticide Selection Offered by: Successful Farming	Apple, TRS	$ 125
Junior Crop Package Offered by: Farmplan	Apple, TI	$ 395
The Landhandler (precision land forming) Offered by: Farm Information Services, Inc.	Apple	$ 275
Level 2 Crop Management (includes Level 1 system) Offered by: Reaper Software Company, Inc.	Apple	$1295
Microbiz Irrigation Mgt. Program Offered by: Micro Business Consulting	TRS	$ 995
Payroll (specialized to crops) Offered by: Agri-Management Services, Inc.	CPM, IBM	$ 595
Seed Corn Dealer Offered by: Computerized Farm Info. Systems, Inc.	Apple	$ 750
Soybeans Crop Disk (irrigation) Offered by: Climate Assessment Technology, Inc.	Apple, TRS, IBM	$ 245
Soybeans Crop Disk (non-irrigation) Offered by: Climate Assessment Technology, Inc.	Apple, TRS, IBM	$ 125
Spring Wheat Crop Disk (irrigation) Offered by: Climate Assessment Technology, Inc.	Apple, TRS, IBM	$ 245
Spring Wheat Crop Disk (non- irrigation) Offered by: Climate Assessment Technology, Inc.	Apple, TRS, IBM	$ 125
Winter Wheat Crop Disk (irrigation) Offered by: Climate Assessment Technology, Inc.	Apple, TRS, IBM	$ 245

Title (Description) and Vendor	Operating System or Computer	Approx. Price
Winter Wheat Crop Disk (non- irrigation) Offered by: Climate Assessment Technology, Inc.	Apple, TRS, IBM	$ 125

— Livestock —

Accounting (re: auctions) Offered by: Agri-Management Services, Inc.	CPM, IBM	$ 595
Accounting (specialized to cattle) Offered by: Agri-Management Services, Inc.	CPM, IBM	$ 595
Accounting (specialized to feedlot) Offered by: Agri-Management Services, Inc.	CPM, IBM	$ 595
Accounting (specialized to swine) Offered by: Agri-Management Services, Inc.	CPM, IBM	$ 595
Beef Cow Management Offered by: Agri-Management Services, Inc.	CPM, IBM	$1995
Beef Enterprise w/Herd Health Offered by: Farm Management Systems of Mississippi, Inc.	IBM	$1000
Beef Gain Projection Offered by: Picton Farm Computers *16K or larger*	TRS	$ 25
Beef Management Analysis Offered by: Ag-tronics Associates	Apple	$ 150
Beef Producer Offered by: Decision Data & Services, Inc.	Apple	$ 700
Beef Projection Offered by: Oklahoma State U. Dept. of Ag. Econ.	Apple, TRS	$ 20
Beef Ration Offered by: Oklahoma State U. Dept. of Ag. Econ.	Apple, TRS	$ 10

Title (Description) and Vendor	Operating System or Computer	Approx. Price
Best Cost Feed Formulation Offered by: Micro-Crop	Apple, TRS, CPM, IBM	$2500
The Big Pork Producer Special Offered by: Farm Information Services, Inc.	Apple	$1255
Boar Selection Program Offered by: Agri-Management Services, Inc.	CPM, IBM	$ 495
Boarding-Training Operation Offered by: Agri-Management Services, Inc.	CPM, IBM	$ 995
Bull Performance Test Offered by: Hi-Plains Systems, Inc.	CPM, IBM, Victor	$ 150
Bull Selection Program Offered by: Agri-Management Services, Inc.	CPM, IBM	$ 495
Cattle Management Offered by: Dalex Computer Systems, Inc.	Apple, IBM	$1125
Commercial Cow/Calf Offered by: Farm Management Systems of Mississippi, Inc.	IBM	$1000
Commercial Cow/Calf Offered by: Hi-Plains Systems, Inc.	CPM, IBM, Victor	$ 295
Commercial Cow/Calf Beef Enterprise Offered by: Farm Management Systems of Mississippi, Inc.	Datamaster	$2000
Commercial Feedlot Program Offered by: Hi-Plains Systems, Inc.	CPM, IBM, Victor	$ 695
Commercial + Feedlot Program Offered by: Hi-Plains Systems, Inc.	CPM, IBM, Victor	$ 995
Cow-Calf Management Offered by: Harris Technical Systems	Apple, IBM, Digital	$ 95
Cow/Calf Planning Offered by: Homestead Computer Company	Vector Graphic, IBM	$ 125

Title (Description) and Vendor	Operating System or Computer	Approx. Price
Cow/Calf Recordkeeping Offered by: Homestead Computer Company	Vector Graphic, IBM	$ 375
Custom Feedlot Program Offered by: Hi-Plains Systems, Inc.	CPM, IBM, Victor	$1995
Dairy Cattle Recordkeeping System Offered by: Computer Consultants	TRS	$ 200
Embryo Transfer Program Offered by: Agri-Management Services, Inc. *need dairy, beef, swine program*	CPM, IBM	$7995
Feed Cost Optimizer System Offered by: Essar Associates	Apple	$ 125
Feed Formulator Offered by: Oklahoma State U. Dept. of Ag. Econ.	Apple, TRS	$ 30
Feed-Miser (records & ration control) Offered by: Decision Data & Services, Inc.	Apple	$ 650
Feed Rationing Mixit-1 Offered by: Agricultural Software Consultants	TRS, CPM, IBM	$ 149
Feed Rationing Mixit-2 Offered by: Agricultural Software Consultants	TRS, CPM, IBM	$ 395
Feeder Cattle Offered by: Harvest Computer Systems	Apple	$ 80
Feeder Pig Cost Offered by: Fred's Micro-ware	Apple, TRS	$ 25
Feedlot Offered by: Oklahoma State U. Dept. of Ag. Econ.	TRS	$ 100
Feedlot (management) Offered by: Agri-Management Services, Inc.	CPM, IBM	$1195
Feedlot Cattle Management Offered by: Harris Technical Systems	Apple, IBM, Digital	$ 95

Title (Description) and Vendor	Operating System or Computer	Approx. Price
Feedlot Planning Offered by: Homestead Computer Company	Vector Graphic, IBM	$ 225
Feedlot Recordkeeping Offered by: Homestead Computer Company	Vector Graphic, IBM	$ 475
Feedlot System Offered by: Micro-Crop	Apple, TRS, CPM, IBM	$2500
Finishing Program for Swine Offered by: Agri-Management Services, Inc.	CPM, IBM	$1195
Foal Management Program Offered by: Agri-Management Services, Inc.	CPM, IBM	$ 995
Herd Audit 2.2 (swine) Offered by: FBS Systems	Apple, TRS, CPM, IBM, TI	$ 595
Hog Farrow to Finish Offered by: Homestead Computer Company	Vector Graphic, IBM	$ 695
Hog Farrowing Records Offered by: Homestead Computer Company	Vector Graphic, IBM	$ 375
Hog Finishing Offered by: Hi-Plains Systems, Inc.	CPM, IBM, Victor	$ 295
Hog Finishing Records Offered by: Homestead Computer Company	Vector Graphic, IBM	$ 375
Hog Management Package Offered by: Harvest Computer Systems	Apple, IBM	$ 300
Hog Management System Offered by: Ag-tronics Associates	Apple	$ 150
Hog Planning Records Offered by: Homestead Computer Company	Vector Graphic, IBM	$ 125
Hog Producer Offered by: Decision Data & Services, Inc.	Apple	$ 800

Title (Description) and Vendor	Operating System or Computer	Approx. Price
Hog Recordkeeping—The Hog Business Manager Offered by: Farm Information Services, Inc.	Apple	$ 275
Hog Recordkeeping—Management Aids Offered by: Farm Information Services, Inc.	Apple	$ 95
Hog Recordkeeping—Sow Productivity Index Offered by: Farm Information Services, Inc.	Apple	$ 250
Hog Recordkeeping—Test Data Offered by: Farm Information Services, Inc.	Apple	$ 750
HPS (Hog Production System) Offered by: Cyberia, Inc.	Commodore	$ 150
Individual Animal Record System Offered by: Agri-Management Services, Inc.	CPM, IBM	$ 495
Junior Pig Package Offered by: Farmplan	Apple, TI	$ 395
Least Cost and Optimizing Ration Formulation (specialized to cattle) Offered by: Agri-Management Services, Inc.	CPM, IBM	$1195
Least Cost and Optimizing Ration Formulation (specialized to feedlot) Offered by: Agri-Management Services, Inc.	CPM, IBM	$1195
Least Cost and Optimizing Ration Formulation (specialized to swine) Offered by: Agri-Management Services, Inc.	CPM, IBM	$1195
Least Cost Feed Formulator Offered by: Agratron, Ltd.	Apple, TRS, CPM, IBM	$ 398
Least Cost Feeds—Beef Offered by: Decision Data & Services, Inc.	Apple	$ 225

Title (Description) and Vendor	Operating System or Computer	Approx. Price
Least Cost Feeds—Swine Offered by: Decision Data & Services, Inc.	Apple	$ 225
Least Cost Nutrition Offered by: Farm Management Systems of Mississippi, Inc.	Datamaster	$2000
Least Cost Nutrition (for small feed mills) Offered by: Farm Management Systems of Mississippi, Inc.	IBM	$1000
Least Cost Rationing Offered by: Farmplan	Apple, TI	$ 225
Litter Management Program Offered by: Agri-Management Services, Inc.	CPM, IBM	$ 495
Livestock Auction (mgt. for auctions) Offered by: Agri-Management Services, Inc.	CPM, IBM	$2995
Livestock Breakeven Analysis Offered by: Hobar Publications	Apple	$ 60
Livestock Decision Aids Offered by: Red Wing Business Systems	Apple, TRS, IBM	$ 75
Livestock Decisions Offered by: Successful Farming	Apple, TRS	$ 89
Livestock Management Offered by: Micro Learningware	Apple, TRS	$ 99
Livestock Package #1 Offered by: Texas Agricultural Extension Service *Texans price*	CPM	$ 25
Livestock Production Analysis Offered by: Ag-Com	Apple	$ 50
Mare Management Offered by: Agri-Management Services, Inc.	CPM, IBM	$2995
Micro-Mixer (least-cost ration program) Offered by: FBS Systems	Apple, TRS, CPM, TI	$ 350

Title (Description) and Vendor	Operating System or Computer	Approx. Price
Order Entry & Receivables (re: auctions) Offered by: Agri-Management Services, Inc.	CPM, IBM	$1195
Pasprojection (gains from pasture for beef cattle) Offered by: Oklahoma State U. Dept. of Ag. Econ.	TRS	$ 20
Payroll (re: auctions) Offered by: Agri-Management Services, Inc.	CPM, IBM	$ 595
Payroll (specialized to cattle) Offered by: Agri-Management Services, Inc.	CPM, IBM	$ 595
Payroll (specialized to feedlot) Offered by: Agri-Management Services, Inc.	CPM, IBM	$ 595
Payroll (specialized to swine) Offered by: Agri-Management Services, Inc.	CPM, IBM	$ 595
Pig Package Offered by: Farmplan	Apple, TI	$ 950
The Pigs Package Offered by: Lloyd's of Bellevue	TRS	$1200
Polled Hereford Cow/Calf Offered by: Hi-Plains Systems, Inc.	CPM, IBM, Victor	$ 495
The Pork Producer Special Offered by: Farm Information Services, Inc.	Apple	$ 995
Private Feedlot Program Offered by: Hi-Plains Systems, Inc.	CPM, IBM, Victor	$ 295
Pro-Hog Manager Offered by: Hi-Plains Systems, Inc.	CPM, IBM, Victor	$ 595
Professional Ration Package Offered by: Agricultural Computer Applications	Apple, TRS, CPM	$3995
Purebred Beef Management Offered by: Farm Management Systems of Mississippi, Inc.	Datamaster	$2000

Title (Description) and Vendor	Operating System or Computer	Approx. Price
Purebred Cow/Calf with Embryo Transplant Offered by: Hi-Plains Systems, Inc.	CPM, IBM, Victor	$ 595
Ranch Package Offered by: Ag-tronics Associates	Apple	$ 50
Ration Formulation Offered by: Dalex Computer Systems, Inc.	Apple, IBM	$ 625
Semen Inventory Offered by: Hi-Plains Systems, Inc.	CPM, IBM, Victor	$ 100
Simmental Cow/Calf Offered by: Hi-Plains Systems, Inc.	CPM, IBM, Victor	$ 495
Sow Audit 2.2 (sow herd) Offered by: FBS Systems	Apple, TRS, CPM, IBM, TI	$ 695
Sow Management Offered by: Agri-Management Services, Inc.	CPM, IBM	$1195
Sow Program Offered by: Fred's Micro-ware	Apple, TRS	$ 100
Stallion Management Offered by: Agri-Management Services, Inc.	CPM, IBM	$ 995
Stocker/Feeder Program Offered by: Hi-Plains Systems, Inc.	CPM, IBM, Victor	$ 395
Stud Farm Accounting Offered by: Agri-Management Services, Inc. *need mare program*	CPM, IBM	$ 995
Swine Cash Flows Offered by: Agratron, Ltd.	Apple, TRS, CPM, IBM	$ 235
Swine Enterprise with Rations Offered by: Computerized Farm Info. Systems, Inc.	Apple, IBM	$ 500
Swine Farrowing Offered by: Harris Technical Systems	Apple, IBM, Digital	$ 95
Swine Feed Offered by: Computerized Farm Info. Systems, Inc.	Apple, IBM	$ 250

Title (Description) and Vendor	Operating System or Computer	Approx. Price
Swine Finishing Offered by: Harris Technical Systems	Apple, IBM, Digital	$ 95
Swine Herd Management Offered by: Computer Agri-Venture	Apple	$ 695
Swine Management Offered by: Farm Management Systems of Mississippi, Inc.	IBM	$1000
Swine Management Offered by: Farm Management Systems of Mississippi, Inc.	Datamaster	$2000
Swine Management—B.O.A.R.S. (pen version) Offered by: Computerized Farm Info. Systems, Inc.	Apple, IBM	$1250
Swine Management—B.O.A.R.S. (stall version) Offered by: Computerized Farm Info. Systems, Inc.	Apple, IBM	$1250
Swine Management Series I Offered by: Harris Technical Systems	Apple, IBM, Digital	$ 155
Swine Management System Offered by: Farmhand Computer Systems, Inc.	CPM	$ 995
Swine Record Keeping Offered by: Harris Technical Systems	Apple, IBM, Digital	$ 650
Swine Records System Offered by: Agratron, Ltd.	Apple, TRS, CPM, IBM	$ 398
Weekly Swine Performance and Management Report Offered by: Agratron, Ltd.	Apple, TRS, CPM, IBM	$ 298

— Equipment/Supplies —

Accounting (re: equip./supply) Offered by: Agri-Management Services, Inc.	CPM, IBM	$ 595
Ag Sprayer Calibration Offered by: Farm Information Services, Inc.	Apple	$ 35

Title (Description) and Vendor	Operating System or Computer	Approx. Price
Equipment Offered by: Compufarm	CPM	$1200
Equipment Management Program Offered by: Agri-Management Services, Inc.	CPM, IBM	$ 495
Farm Equipment & Parts Dealer Offered by: Micro-Crop	Apple, TRS, CPM, IBM	$3250
Farm Fleet Operations Offered by: Micro-Crop	Apple, TRS, CPM, IBM	$4750
Farm Supplies Management Offered by: Micro-Crop	Apple, TRS, CPM, IBM	$ 650
Farm Vehicles & Machinery Offered by: Micro-Crop	Apple, TRS, CPM, IBM	$1500
Inventory (re: equipment/supply) Offered by: Agri-Management Services, Inc.	CPM, IBM	$1195
Irrigator Offered by: Ag-tronics Associates	Apple	$ 100
Irrigator II Offered by: Ag-tronics Associates	Apple	$ 200
Machine Cost Offered by: Oklahoma State U. Dept. of Ag. Econ.	Apple, TRS	$ 10
Machinery Cost Management Offered by: Picton Farm Computers *16K or larger*	TRS	$ 25
Machinery Management Offered by: Harris Technical Systems	Apple, IBM, Digital	$ 95
Machinery Management Series I Offered by: Harris Technical Systems	Apple, IBM, Digital	$ 155

Order Entry & Receivables (re:
  equipment/supply)
Offered by: Agri-Management
  Services, Inc.
	CPM, IBM	$1195

Parts Inventory Offered by: Farm Information Services, Inc.	Apple	$ 95

Title (Description) and Vendor	Operating System or Computer	Approx. Price
Payroll (re: equip./supply) Offered by: Agri-Management Services, Inc.	CPM, IBM	$ 595
PM-Status II (equipment maintenance) Offered by: Anawan Computer Services	TRS, CPM, IBM	$ 395
Tractor Selection (using Neb. test data) Offered by: Hobar Publications	Apple	$ 40
— Poultry —		
Accounting (specialized to poultry) Offered by: Agri-Management Services, Inc.	CPM, IBM	$ 595
Broiler Sales Controller Offered by: Agrimetrics Associates	Apple	$ 375
Commercial Layer Controller Offered by: Agrimetrics Associates	Apple	$ 250
Commercial Pullet Controller Offered by: Agrimetrics Associates	Apple	$ 200
ECI (Egg Clearinghouse) Receive Terminal Offered by: Locus Systems	TRS	$ 30
Egg Production/Pricing (for egg processors) Offered by: Locus Systems	Apple, TRS	$ 135
Feed Manufacturer's Controller Offered by: Agrimetrics Associates	Apple	$ 150
Flock Service Report Offered by: Locus Systems	Apple, TRS	$ 30
Grade Out Analysis Offered by: Locus Systems	Apple, TRS	$ 30
Grower (poultry) Offered by: Agri-Management Services, Inc.	CPM, IBM	$1995
Layer (poultry) Offered by: Agri-Management Services, Inc.	CPM, IBM	$1995

Title (Description) and Vendor	Operating System or Computer	Approx. Price
Laying Breeder Controller Offered by: Agrimetrics Associates	Apple	$ 250
Least Cost and Optimizing Ration Formulation (specialized to poultry) Offered by: Agri-Management Services, Inc.	CPM, IBM	$1195
Least Cost Feed Formulation Offered by: Agrimetrics Associates	Apple	$ 975
Monthly Feed Consumed Offered by: Locus Systems	Apple, TRS	$ 20
Nest Run Val-U-Calc (grade or sell eggs nest run) Offered by: Agrimetrics Associates	Apple	$ 150
Payroll (specialized to poultry) Offered by: Agri-Management Services, Inc.	CPM, IBM	$ 595
Production Cash Flow Offered by: Locus Systems	Apple, TRS	$ 100
Pullet Breeder Controller Offered by: Agrimetrics Associates	Apple	$ 200
Turkey Enterprise Offered by: Computerized Farm Info. Systems, Inc.	Apple	$ 500
Weekly Egg Production & Livability Tracking Offered by: Locus Systems	Apple, TRS	$ 30
Weekly Feed Consumed Offered by: Locus Systems	Apple, TRS	$ 30

– Other –

Accounting (re: feed plant) Offered by: Agri-Management Services, Inc.	CPM, IBM	$ 595
Accounting (re: fertilizer) Offered by: Agri-Management Services, Inc.	CPM, IBM	$ 595

Title (Description) and Vendor	Operating System or Computer	Approx. Price
Accounting (re: grove & orchard) Offered by: Agri-Management Services, Inc.	CPM, IBM	$ 595
Accounting (re: plant nursery) Offered by: Agri-Management Services, Inc.	CPM, IBM	$ 595
Action List & Business Cards Offered by: Farm Information Services, Inc.	Apple	$ 50
Ag-Marketer Offered by: Countryside Data	Apple	$ 350
Agricultural Market & Commodities Futures Offered by: Fred's Micro-ware	Apple, TRS	$ 50
Agricultural Marketing & Commodity Futures Offered by: Hobar Publications	Apple	$ 50
Agricultural Marketing/Commodity Future Offered by: Micro Learningware	Apple	$ 50
Bee Hive Management & Inventory Control Offered by: George K. Snell	TRS	$ 70
Chanl (marketing—channel breakout—trend follow) Offered by: Micro Futures	Apple, TRS, IBM	$ 125
Chart Master (commodities) Offered by: Decision Data & Services, Inc.	Apple	$ 550
Charting for Profit (commodities analysis) Offered by: Successful Farming	Apple, TRS	$ 225
Chartmaster (commodities analysis) Offered by: Professional Farm Software	Apple, TRS, IBM	$ 400
Chartpac (charting software) Offered by: Micro Futures	Apple, TRS	$ 100

Title (Description) and Vendor	Operating System or Computer	Approx. Price
Colorite (graphic draw program) Offered by: Picton Farm Computers *4K or larger*	TRS	$ 15
Comdata (commodities/marketing records) Offered by: Micro Futures	Apple, TRS, IBM	$ 125
(Commodity Futures Data Retrieval) MJK Access Offered by: Micro Futures	Apple, TRS	$ 75
Dirind (oscillator—net change in price) Offered by: Micro Futures	Apple, TRS, IBM	$ 125
DRF (price movement oscillator— trend/countertrend) Offered by: Micro Futures	Apple, TRS, IBM	$ 125
Farmfiler (record filing system) Offered by: Farmplan	Apple	$ 225
Farmfiler Models (preformatted record models) Offered by: Farmplan	Apple	$ 55
Farmi Micro Manager Computer System (total system) Offered by: OT Industries, Inc.	Farmi	$2995
Fertilizer Dealer (mgt. of dealerships) Offered by: Micro-Crop	Apple, TRS, CPM, IBM	$4000
Florist Offered by: Micro-Crop	Apple, TRS, CPM, IBM	$3000
Forest Inventory Analysis Offered by: Duane Bristow—Albany, Ky.	TRS	$ 55
Forest Sample Database Offered by: Duane Bristow—Albany, Ky.	TRS	$ 195
Grove & Orchard (mgt.) Offered by: Agri-Management Services, Inc.	CPM, IBM	$ 995
Inventory (re: feed plant) Offered by: Agri-Management Services, Inc.	CPM, IBM	$1195

Title (Description) and Vendor	Operating System or Computer	Approx. Price
Inventory (re: fertilizer) Offered by: Agri-Management Services, Inc.	CPM, IBM	$1195
Inventory (re: plant nursery) Offered by: Agri-Management Services, Inc.	CPM, IBM	$1195
Investment Analysis Program (forestry programs) Offered by: Forestry Supplies	Apple, TRS, IBM, TI	$ 300
Land Leveling Offered by: Agdata	TRS, CPM, Vector Graphic, IBM	$ 750
Land Purchase Offered by: Ag Plus Software	Apple	$ 50
Least Cost & Optimizing Ration Formulation (re: feed plant) Offered by: Agri-Management Services, Inc.	CPM, IBM	$1195
Least Cost or Optimizing Fertilizer Formulation Offered by: Agri-Management Services, Inc.	CPM, IBM	$1195
LSO (lagged, high/low chanl. brkout. w/$ stop loss) Offered by: Micro Futures	Apple, TRS, IBM	$ 125
M-II (lagged, high/low price brkout., reverse system) Offered by: Micro Futures	Apple, TRS, IBM	$ 125
Maband (moving average—trend following) Offered by: Micro Futures	Apple, TRS, IBM	$ 125
Macross (moving average crossover system) Offered by: Micro Futures	Apple, TRS, IBM	$ 125
Magnum Research System (trading system research) Offered by: Micro Futures	Apple, TRS, IBM	$ 800
Mailing List Offered by: Farm Information Services, Inc.	Apple	$ 175

Title (Description) and Vendor	Operating System or Computer	Approx. Price
Mailit (mailing list system) Offered by: Duane Bristow—Albany, Ky.	TRS	$ 60
Market Charting Package Offered by: Harris Technical Systems	Apple, IBM	$ 450
Market Trend Offered by: Fred's Micro-ware	Apple, TRS	$ 25
Market Trend Charting (commodities analysis) Offered by: Micro Learningware	TRS	$ 20
Market Window (commodities) Offered by: FBS Systems	TRS, IBM	$ 995
MO (momentum index using two MA's) Offered by: Micro Futures	Apple, TRS, IBM	$ 125
Modterm (communications program) Offered by: Micro Spike	CPM	$ 60
Nurseryman Offered by: Micro-Crop	Apple, TRS, CPM, IBM	$3000
Order Entry & Receivables (re: feed plant) Offered by: Agri-Management Services, Inc.	CPM, IBM	$1195
Order Entry & Receivables (re: fertilizer) Offered by: Agri-Management Services, Inc.	CPM, IBM	$1195
OS (moving average oscillator—trend/countertrend) Offered by: Micro Futures	Apple, TRS, IBM	$ 125
Payroll (re: feed plant) Offered by: Agri-Management Services, Inc.	CPM, IBM	$ 595
Payroll (re: fertilizer) Offered by: Agri-Management Services, Inc.	CPM, IBM	$ 595

Title (Description) and Vendor	Operating System or Computer	Approx. Price
Payroll (re: grove & orchard) Offered by: Agri-Management Services, Inc.	CPM, IBM	$ 595
Payroll (re: plant nursery) Offered by: Agri-Management Services, Inc.	CPM, IBM	$1195
Plant Nursery Management Offered by: Agri-Management Services, Inc.	CPM, IBM	$ 995
Plot/Point Sample Program (forestry programs) Offered by: Forestry Supplies	Apple, TRS, IBM, TI	$ 400
Portfolio Mgt. Software Offered by: Micro Futures *need 132-col. printer*	Apple, TRS	$ 295
Ranqo (oscillator—average change in price) Offered by: Micro Futures	Apple, TRS, IBM	$ 125
Schedule (recurring & non-recurring events) Offered by: Compufarm	CPM	$ 600
Surveying Calculations Offered by: Duane Bristow—Albany, Ky.	TRS	$ 250
Text Editor Offered by: Duane Bristow—Albany, Ky.	TRS	$ 70
Timber Base—100% Cruise Offered by: Duane Bristow—Albany, Ky.	TRS	$ 195
Voc-Ag Enterprise Offered by: Decision Data & Services, Inc.	Apple	$ 150
Weather Station Data Analysis Offered by: Micro-Crop	Apple, TRS, CPM, IBM	$3000
Writsit (letter-writing system) Offered by: Duane Bristow—Albany, Ky.	TRS	$ 60

Title (Description) and Vendor	Operating System or Computer	Approx. Price
– Dairy –		
ACA Complete Feed Ration Formulation Offered by: Dairy Herd Management Services, Inc.	Apple, TRS, CPM, Victor, IBM, Altos	$1995
Calf Management Program Offered by: Agri-Management Services, Inc.	CPM, IBM	$ 495
Comprehensive Dairy Nutrition System (5 programs) Offered by: Del Burnett & Associates	TRS	$ 900
Consultation/Support Service (for nutrition system) Offered by: Del Burnett & Associates	TRS	$1200
Dairy & Beef Data Disk for Mixit-2 Offered by: Agricultural Software Consultants	TRS, CPM, IBM	$ 50
Dairy Cattle Least Cost Ration Program Offered by: Agricultural Software Consultants	TRS, CPM, IBM	$ 445
Dairy Cow Offered by: Oklahoma State U. Dept. of Ag. Econ.	Apple, TRS	$ 12
Dairy Cow Management Offered by: Agri-Management Services, Inc.	CPM, IBM	$1995
Dairy Diary Offered by: FBS Systems	TRS	$ 695
Dairy Herd & Health Management Offered by: Farm Management Systems of Mississippi, Inc.	IBM	$1000
Dairy Herd and Health Management Systems Offered by: IBM	Datamaster	$2000
Dairy Herd Management Offered by: Countryside Data V	CPM	$ 995

Title (Description) and Vendor	Operating System or Computer	Approx. Price
Dairy Herd Management (by Countryside) Offered by: Countryside Data	CPM	$ 500
Dairy Herd Management DairyCalc Templates Offered by: Dairy Herd Management Services, Inc.	Apple, TRS, CPM, Victor, IBM, Altos	$ 200
Dairy Herd Management System / Level III Offered by: Dairy Herd Management Services, Inc.	Apple, TRS, CPM, Victor, IBM, Altos	$2995
Dairy Journal Offered by: Harvest Computer Systems	Apple	$ 600
Dairy Management Offered by: Computerized Farm Info. Systems, Inc.	Apple, IBM	$1050
Dairy Management Offered by: Farm Management Systems of Mississippi, Inc.	IBM	$1000
Dairy Package Offered by: Farmplan	Apple, TI	$ 950
Dairy Ration Evaluation Offered by: Agricultural Computer Applications	Apple, TRS, CPM	$ 495
Dairy Ration Formulation Offered by: Agricultural Computer Applications	Apple, TRS, CPM	$1995
Do It (time management) Offered by: Micro Spike	CPM	$ 250
Feedlot Management (custom feedlots) Offered by: Dairy Herd Management Services, Inc.	Apple, TRS, CPM, Victor, IBM, Altos	$5000
Food Inventory Offered by: Dairy Herd Management Services, Inc.	Apple, TRS, CPM, Victor, IBM, Altos	$1095
Herd Management 5S Offered by: Countryside Data	CPM	$1250

Title (Description) and Vendor	Operating System or Computer	Approx. Price
Individualized Training (for nutrition system) Offered by: Del Burnett & Associates	TRS	$ 500
Inventory Offered by: Micro Spike	CPM	$ 500
Junior Dairy Package Offered by: Farmplan	Apple, TI	$ 395
Least Cost & Optimizing Ration Formulation (specialized to dairy) Offered by: Agri-Management Services, Inc.	CPM, IBM	$1195
Milk Program (daily milk weights records) Offered by: Micro Spike	CPM	$ 600
Pedigree Program (prepare 3 generations animals) Offered by: Micro Spike	CPM	$ 100
Produce Packing Tracking Offered by: Dairy Herd Management Services, Inc.	Apple, TRS, CPM, Victor, IBM, Altos	$1095
Ration Balancer Template Offered by: Micro Spike	CPM	$ 30
Revision/Enhancement Service (for nutrition system) Offered by: Del Burnett & Associates	TRS	$ 400
Sire Selection Program Offered by: Agri-Management Services, Inc.	CPM, IBM	$ 495
Sort Program (ranks cow by quality) Offered by: Micro Spike	CPM	$ 100
Treatment (vet work / breeding info.) Offered by: Micro Spike	CPM	$ 250
Treatment Summary Offered by: Micro Spike	CPM	$ 100

— *Educational* —

Ag-Finance (educational) Offered by: Countryside Data	CPM	$ 250

Title (Description) and Vendor	Operating System or Computer	Approx. Price
Ag-Marketer (educational) Offered by: Countryside Data	Apple	$ 300
Ag-Planner (educational) Offered by: Countryside Data	CPM	$ 175
Agricultural Machinery & Related Review Offered by: Hobar Publications	Apple	$ 30
Commodore 64 Tutorial (Volume I) Offered by: Cyberia, Inc.	Commodore	$ 25
Corn and Soybean Review Offered by: Hobar Publications	Apple	$ 30
Dairy Herd Management (Countryside) (educ.) Offered by: Countryside Data	CPM	$ 300
Dairy Herd Management (Marshall) (educ.) Offered by: Countryside Data	CPM	$ 350
F.A.R.M. Educational (for use by high schools) Offered by: Specialized Data Systems, Inc.	Apple	$ 250
F.A.R.M. Probs. on Dairy/Swine/Beef/ Cash Grain Offered by: Hobar Publications	Apple	$ 50
Farm Acct. & Records Mgt.— Commercial Package Offered by: Hobar Publications	Apple	$ 395
Milk Let Down Offered by: Hobar Publications	Apple	$ 30

APPENDIX C

Vendors

Ag Plus Software
906 S. Main St.
Ida Grove, IA 51445
712/364-2135

Ag-Com
Box 706
Muscatine, IA 52761
319/263-8475

Agdata
891 Hazel St.
Gridley, CA 95948
916/846-6203

Ag-Data, Inc.
P.O. Box 672
Walla Walla, WA 99362
509/525-2580

Agratron, Ltd.
6914 Dillon
Houston, TX 77061
713/641-1255

Agricultural Computer Applications,
   Inc.
P.O. Box 8
Davis, CA 95617
916/756-8946

Agricultural Software Consultants
1706 Sante Fe
Kingsville, TX 78363
512/595-1937

Agri-Data Systems
2432 W. Peoria, Suite 1323
Phoenix, AZ 85029
602/955-5158

Agri-Management Services, Inc.
P.O. Box 3659
Logan, UT 84321
801/753-7209

Agrimetrics Associates, Inc.
P.O. Box 34190
Richmond, VA 23234
804/748-8176

Ag-tronics Associates
143 E. 300 North St.
Hyde Park, UT 84318
801/563-3701

Altamont Computers, Inc.
807 Central Ave.
Tracy, CA 95376
209/836-2400

Amec, Inc.
315 Haggerty Lane
Bozeman, MT 59715
406/586-0548

Anawan Computer Services
19 Winterberry Lane
Rehoboth, MA 02769
619/252-4537

Anthro Digital, Inc.
103 Bartlett Ave.
Pittsfield, MA 01201
413/448-8278

Duane Bristow
Rt. 3, Box 444C
Albany, KY 42602
606/387-5884

Broderbund Software, Inc.
1938 Fourth St.
San Rafael, CA 94901
415/456-6424

157

Brubaker & Associates, Inc.
116 W. Main St.
Delphi, IN 46923
317/564-2584

Del Burnett and Associates
668 E. Main St.
Versailles, OH 45380
513/526-5809

Chadwick Company
9789 Cavell Circle
Bloomington, MN 55438
612/388-2691

Climate Assessment Technology,
   Inc.
11550 Fuqua St., Suite 355
Houston, TX 77034
713/484-3603

Comm Basic, Inc., Assoc.
7920 Chambersburg Road
Dayton, OH 45424
513/233-9904

Compu Trac, Inc.
P.O. Box 15951
New Orleans, LA 70115
800/535-7990

Compufarm
Advanced Business Microsystems
P.O. Box 9352
Marina Del Rey, CA 92091
213/823-7055

Computer Agri-Venture
105 S. 3rd St.
St. Peter, MN 56082
507/931-6060

Computer Consultants
Box 6686-L
Marietta, GA 30065
404/971-4422

Computerized Farm Information
   System
1710 Oldridge Ave.
P.O. Box 302
Stillwater, MN 55082
612/436-7198

Comput-R-Systems
Dale Hutchinson
10818 Brentway Drive
Houston, TX 77070
713/496-2584

Comtech
Box 699
Riverside, ND 58078
701/282-6894

Countryside Data, Inc.
718 N. Skyline Drive, Suite 201
Idaho Falls, ID 83402
208/529-8576

Cyberia, Inc.
2330 Lincoln Way
Ames, IA 50010
515/292-7634

Dairy Herd Mgt. Service, Inc.
715 S. Bank Road
Elma, WA 98541
206/482-4073

Dalex Computer Systems, Inc.
4725 Island View Drive
Mound, MN 55364
612/472-1273

Decision Data and Services, Inc.
538 S. Duff
Ames, IA 50010
515/233-4873

Educational Performance System,
   Inc.
309 Office Plaza, Suite 204
Tallahassee, FL 32308
904/878-7308

Electronic Service
Box 128
Mansfield, IL 61854
217/489-3241

Essar Associates
6545 Zebra Court
West Chester, OH 45069
513/777-8339

F.A.R.M. Computer Consulting
Rich or Judy Olson
Rt. 1, Box 93
Garfield, WA 99130
509/635-1448

Farm Computer System
Greg Downs
RR 2
Hillsboro, ND 58045
701/436-5757

Farm Info. Services
P.O. Box 336
Waterproof, LA 71375
318/749-5535

Farm Management Systems
1208 S. Cedar
New Lenox, IL 60451
815/485-4955

Farm Management Systems of
  Mississippi, Inc.
P.O. Box 646
McComb, MS 39648
601/684-8394

Farmhand Computer Systems, Ltd.
Box 40
Mitchellville, IA 50169
515/967-7220

Farmplan Computer System, Inc.
1055 Sunnyvale Saratoga Road,
  No. 1
Sunnyvale, CA 94087
408/746-0636

FBS Systems
P.O. Box 201
Aledo, IL 61231
309/582-5628

Financial Systems, Inc.
P.O. Box 2012
Kearney, NE 68847
308/237-5998

Forestry Suppliers
P.O. Box 8397
Jackson, MS 39204
601/354-3565

Fred's Micro-ware
Fred Rennpferd
Box 162, Rt. 1
Amboy, MN 56010
507/674-3068

Frontier Computer Corporation
2630 W. Durham Ferry Road
Tracy, CA 95376
209/836-2098

Harris Technical Systems
624 Peach St.
P.O. Box 80837
Lincoln, NE 68501
402/476-2811

Harvest Computer Systems, Inc.
102 S. Harrison St.
Alexandria, IN 46001
317/724-9527

E F Haskell & Associates, Inc.
1528 E. Missouri, Suite A131
Phoenix, AZ 85014
602/277-2534

H.C.I.
1115 W. Hwy. 7
Hutchinson, MN 55350
612/587-2940

Hi-Plains Systems, Inc.
P.O. Box 8152
Amarillo, TX 79109
806/353-3421

Hobar Publications
1234 Tiller Lane
St. Paul, MN 55112
612/633-3170
612/633-1630

Homestead Computer Company
2530 Crawford Ave., Suite 317
Evanston, IL 60201
312/864-6777

Iowa Farm Business Association
P.O. Box 1809
Ames, IA 50010
515/233-5802

International Business Machines
General Systems Division
411 Northside Parkway, N.W.
P.O. Box 2150
Atlanta, GA 30327
404/238-2000

Linden Fielding
Rt. #2, Box 248
Shelley, ID 83274
208/357-7751

Lloyd's of Bellevue
1004 Durand Drive
Bellevue, NE 68005
402/291-4028

Locus Systems
Chick Haven Feed Service, Inc.
P.O. Box 248
North Wilkesboro, NC 28659
919/838-4166

McIntosh Software
987 14th St.
Marion, IA 52302
319/377-9341

Micro Business Consulting
111 S. Locust
Visalia, CA 93291
209/625-4597

Micro Futures
Jeffrey A. Miller
P.O. Box 2765
Livonia, MI 48154
313/422-0914

Micro Learningware
Hwy. 66 South, Box 307
Mankato, MN 56002-0307
507/625-2205

Micro Mike's, Inc.
3015 Plains Blvd.
Amarillo, TX 79102
806/372-3633

Micro Spike
8400 N. Seymour Road
Owosso, MI 48867
517/725-6527

Micro-Crop
8245 NW 53 St.
Miami, FL 33166
305/594-2925

Oklahoma State University
Ted R. Nelson
513 Ag Hall
Stillwater, OK 74078
405/624-6081

On-Farm Computing, Inc.
5950 W. Raymond St.
Indianapolis, IN 46241
317/247-5179

OT Industries, Inc.
332 Chester St.
St. Paul, MN 55107
612/227-3174

Panamint Data Systems
1400 Easton Drive, Suite 103
Bakersfield, CA 93309
805/327-0055

Pearlsoft
Relational Systems Intl. Corp.
3700 River Road N.
Salem, OR 97303
506/390-6880

Owen Picton
Picton Farm Computers
Rt. 3
Blair, NE 68008
402/426-5876

Pioneer Hi-Bred Int'l, Inc.
Farm Information Services Division
5880 Merle Hay Road
Johnston, IA 50131
515/270-3557

Plan-A-Farm America
220 Division St.
Northfield, MN 55057
507/645-4411

Professional Farm Software
John Jokerst
219 Parkade
Cedar Falls, IA 50613
319/277-1278

Reaper Software Co., Inc.
808 Olena Ave.
Willmar, MN 56201
612/235-6425

Red Wing Business Systems
610 Main St.
P.O. Box 19
Red Wing, MN 55066
612/388-1106

Edward J. Rolenc
Edward J. Rolenc & Associates
604 E. Henry
Mt. Pleasant, IA 52641
319/385-3290

Shawgo and Associates
P.O. Box 2328
Amarillo, TX 79105
806/376-4284

Small Business Computer Systems
4140 Greenwood
Lincoln, NE 68504
402/467-1878

Smith, Dennis and Gaylord, Inc.
3211 Scott Blvd.
Santa Clara, CA 95051
408/727-1870

George K. Snell
Rt. 1, Box 75
Honor, MI 49640
305/878-5804

Specialized Data Systems, Inc.
P.O. Box 8278
Madison, WI 53708
608/241-5050

Successful Farming Mgt. Software
Locust at 17th
Des Moines, IA 50336
515/284-2916

Summerville Enterprises
104 Broad St., S.E.
Aliceville, AL 35442
205/373-6383

Systems for Management
   Information
Box 38
Strawberry Point, IA 52076
319/933-2296

Terrell Brothers
Rt. 1, Box 69
Woodford, VA 22580-9763
804/448-4655

The Texas A&M University System
Texas Ag. Ext. Serv. & Exp. St.
Room 113, USDA Building
College Station, TX 77843
713/845-3929

Vertical Software, Inc.
502 E. War Memorial Drive
Peoria, IL 61614
309/688-2377

Wisconsin Microware
5201 Old Mikkleton Road
Madison, WI 53705
608/255-9020